Date- 05/30/14

Distributed in United States by

Createspace.com

Copyright 2014 by Jerry Ayers

Printed in the United States of America

New World Order

By Jerry Ayers

Introduction

New world order. Many people have their own theories of what a new world order is. I have one as well but not to control the world but to give it freedom to think for itself. The common New World Order most people worry about is the order that put people back to slavery. The "Control Freaks" come together and combine their power to control every element of this world by changing the laws to their benefits. Their plan is to control everything and to have the inferior group to think in one robotic pattern. In order for them to succeed, the Control Freaks will have to control the education system, television, celebrities and everything that advertise. My plan is to report the solutions to our problems so that we can avoid this humane extinction.

My goal is to expose the things that the masses fail to see by acknowledging the biggest problems that are causing "New World Order" to be successful, though it's already half way through its success. The purpose of this book is to inform the minds to prevent the "New World Order" from happening; the devilish New World Order. After years of researching, I've discovered 11 most important topics that the "Brainwashers" use to control the world. This book will open your eyes and you will learn a better way to live life.

Table of Contents

Chapter 1

Evolution, the key ingredient for

NWO

Evolution, the key ingredient for NWO

First you have to understand the purpose of the evolution theory. This chapter will help you better understand the later chapters in this book. Persons who believe in creation will most likely agree with this book and the persons who believe in evolution will most likely disagree. So I added this chapter to explain the difference and truths about evolution and creation. Know the fact that evolution represents man, while creation represents God. Whether you agree or disagree with me, I speak nothing but common sense and logic. None of these words is for my benefits but for the world's benefits. Please read more

There is no evidence that shows one kind of life turning into another kind. Living things on earth are not seen to be evolving into something else. Dinosaurs suddenly appear into the fossil record, with no links to any ancestors before them. They multiplied greatly but then became extinct. If evolution was a fact, the fossils should reveal beginnings of new structures in living things. There should be fossils with developing arms, legs, wings, eyes and other bones and organs. Humans reproduce only after their own kind, and have always done so today and in the past. Also, Evolution can't explain how lifeless chemicals came alive. What rules of grammar lies behind the genetic code? How genes shape the form of living things? Evolution admit that the probability of the right atoms and molecule is 16 zillion or 1 followed by 132 zeros but for more than 1 simple protein molecule is needed for life. Some 2000 different proteins are need just for a cell to maintain its activity, and the chance that all of them will occur at random is 1 in 10 followed by 40,000! Life and the universe would be impossible if certain design factors were off by even a small fraction. Also, was it chance that placed the earth at just the right distance from the sun, its source of energy in the form of light and heat? Was it chance that caused the earth to move around the sun at just the right speed, to rotate on its axis every 24 years and to have the correct angle or tilt? Was it chance that provide the earth with a protective atmosphere having the right mixture of gases? Was it chance that gave earth water to grow food. Bats uses sonar, Eels make electricity, Gulls desalt water, wasps make paper, Termites install air condition, Octopuses use jet propulsion, birds build houses, ants do gardening or sewing, fireflies with built in flashlights. Could "Chance" have done all of this? All parts of organs have to work together for sight, hearing and thinking to take place. Such organs would have been useless until all individual parts were completed. Could the chance of evolution brought all these parts together at the right time to produce such elaborate mechonamisms?

More Evidence

As our body makes new cells billions of times a day without our conscious guidance, it requires copies of all 3 components- DNA, RNF, and protein. In fact, a Gene holds information needed to build a protein. The sequence of the letters in the Gene forms a coded message or blue print that tells what kind of protein should be built. The DNA, with all its sub units is the master molecule of life. Without its coded instructions, diverse proteins could not exist, thus no life. This is the evidence that point to a creator, which is the vast intelligent, organized universe, including design manifest in our body cells. And third is our brain, with our associated awareness of self and our interest in the future. The human brain is the most complicated and most complex object in the universe. Our brain develops throughout our lifetime by what we allow to enter through our senses and what we choose to think about. We have 5 senses- sight, hearing, smell, tastes, and touch that depend on the human brain. Our brain can hold information that would fill 50 million volumes. During an average life span, a person uses only 1/100 of percent of his potential brain capacity. The human brain can store and recall information, that makes it the most remarkable phenomenon in biological universe. Everything that makes us human- language, thought, knowledge, culture- is the result of a creator not evolution.

WHY DO WE GROW OLD

Some cells in your skin, liver and intestines maybe replaced daily. Every second, your body produces about 25 million new cells as replacements. If this did not happen, you would grow old during childhood. When our cells are regenerated, each new cell must have a copy of your DNA, the molecule that contains much of the information needed to reproduce your entire body. Since all parts of our body from major structures to the tiny molecules are constantly replaced. Wear and tear does not fully explain aging. The body numerous systems repair themselves for decades, each in a different way and at a different pace. Locked within the code of genetic material are instructions that specify the age beyond which a species cannot live. Maximum life span approaches, genes exist which can tell cells and entire organisms to grow old and die. This is clear evidence that there is a creator and the "Brainwashers" don't want you to find out this information.

The purpose of this chapter will help you to develop mentally, emotionally, morally and spiritually, to have faith in overcoming the New World Order. Also, it'll help you understand how Evolution was made up as the key ingredient for the New World Order.

Chapter 2

Solitary combats Brainwashers

Now that you read that chapter, I'm pretty sure we're on the same page now. I want to tell you that self-knowledge comes from solitary by spending time by yourself with just you and your thoughts. Freedom thinking exercises your mind and extends or stretches your thinking power. Solitary is similar to meditation, and Gandhi used that form to gain knowledge. Your brain basically runs through electricity. So when less electricity is around you, the less static (interference) you'll have or the more focus power your electricity will run. In this chapter "Solitary" explains how I began writing this book. I couldn't have written this book without solitary and self-knowledge.

Solitary combats Brainwashers

When I was slipping into the hands of the "Control Freaks" solitary raised me back up and I was able to think for myself.. Solitary helps me clear my conscience and also keeps me focus. Not saying that I'm a loner because I am a people's person, I like to be around people as much I am by myself. That way I'm able to think clearer, come up with ideas, eat better, sing in the shower without feelings of embarrassment and most of all converse with God. When I am alone I talk to God as if someone was standing next to me. I ask Him a lot of questions and talk about random stuff for some time and wait for answers. The reason I like to talk to God throughout the day because I really believe he listens.

I used to have doubt; I used to embrace my own flaws giving myself excuses to be inferior to perfection. But I found and accepted myself through solitary. Never underestimate solitary as it teaches things about yourself. You need to know how to be alone and not defined by another. If you find out you don't like who you are, every new day is a chance to change your life, but don't clone someone else when you change, be all you can be because nobody else wants to be you. If you wonder why you can't shine it's because you're cloning. Remember stars can't shine without darkness, solitary is your darkness for you to see yourself and for everybody to see your shine. This is how I found myself. I became a writer through solitary. I developed a gifted personality, and my own philosophy through solitary. Everything that happened to me in my whole life experiences; I learned to put it in words. The things that my eyes saw, the pain that I felt, the cries that I heard, the shoes that I walked in is the experience I'm using to put in a book to prevent the New World Order.

Chapter 3

Freedom

Freedom

This chapter explains the most important aspect of life; freedom. This part of life is slowly being taken away from us without us knowing. If people do not alert themselves; their freedom of choices will be gone. They won't be able to choose what to eat, what to think, what to learn, who to worship, how to look and soon sexual orientation. The people who want to rule the world are eager to take everything you existed for from you. They want to make the purpose of your life the benefits of their greed. If you're not free to love, free to choose, free to think, then you're not living. In the next few paragraphs explains what freedom is.

Must I say I am proud to be an African American and proud to live in America most likely because of the freedom we possess and the free will to say anything we want. Unfortunately in other countries people would get gunned down, jailed or their head cut off if they would have said the things I have said. But what's good of having freedom when it can get you killed and when no one respects it. In reality freedom only means do what you want until someone kills you because of your belief. Well I guess it depends on how you define freedom and how you use it. Some people use it to offend others and some use it for good purposes. In a country where you can say anything you want except writing the president a threaten letter, people are ignorantly depowering the word "Freedom" which is the reason more laws are being created when more people abuse it. America has spoiled its people by accepting all religions, beliefs and personalities. It's just that half of the people living here don't accept their differences. Well I think people should understand that freedom, real freedom doesn't exist in the same time and same place where racism dominates. Freedom only comes when you die because no one can tell you anything. So if you want to live closest to freedom you must learn to get rid of the hatred that's living in your heart and accept people's differences. All and all freedom of speech could be a good idea for someone but also can be a threat to someone else. Take Note: Remember Kevin Trudeau. Even his freedom of speech sent him to prison because no one wants to hear the truth. The world loves being ignorant. The purpose of this chapter is to notify that you don't have long to enjoy the freedom you think you have until you recognize your own thoughts. You must protect your freedom but knowing what is good and bad for you. If the doctors tell you that you have to take prescription pills for the rest of your life, they are trying to steal your freedom from you. If you don't learn to grow your own food or at least some, you will lose freedom to choose what to put in your mouth. If you don't embrace the freedom you have, you will be easy succumb to the New World Order.

Read this note

I love nature. I adore space, the ocean, the forest and everything else. I have dreams of wandering in the forest, scuba diving and visiting other planets. I stare at the stars whenever they're visible and I imagine. It's the deep appreciation I have for creation. Another thing I do for nature is when I buy apples or any other fruits that has seeds, I never throw the seeds away. Instead I collect them and put it in a plastic bag and send it back to whatever farm it came from. I know farms probably have plenty of apple seeds; I just feel that seeds shouldn't be thrown away. Anything that can grow food shouldn't be thrown in a garbage can; rather it should be mailed to poverty homes. I thought that If God made it poisonous to consume apple or any fruit seeds, it's because the seeds are meant to multiply not to die. I just felt that if we can help nature, then nature can help us. So not only I strive to make this a better America, I strive to make this a better world to live in. I have high hopes of influencing the masses to make their life better. This book is for better understanding, better relationships, better morals, better education, better life and better thinking. God bless.

The point of this note is that we have the mind to be amaze and love creations forever. Our minds are so powerful that it is the only thing that can live outside of nature. It has the ability to create. What we imagine and use into our minds becomes knowledge and knowledge is the seed to life. You throw your seeds away is the same as "a mind is a terrible thing to waste". You can't keep thoughts to yourself as it poisons you physically. Being physical is only a slave to being mental. You have to be a leader of your own mind. Think for yourself.

Chapter 4

Racism/Self Hate

Racism-self hate

Racism and self-hate (people who hate their own kind) is an act of selfishness, lack of appreciation for creation and a sign of ignorance. It is definitely supported by the people who are trying to control the world so that it can control each race of human beings. The key to defeating racism and self-hate is to learn about yourself and your nationality history. Failure to learn about your ethnic history will make you an easy target for self-hate. Overall, Racism is one of the key ingredients to slaving the world by making classes of people. Just look at the ghettos, majority of the ghettos are populated by blacks because the poor are forced to round up into the projects. Money is not spent into those neighborhoods to rebuild because it's their way of keeping those people in that state. Though America being the wealthiest country in the world, they can fix the poor neighborhoods but then again equality would ruin the "New World Order". Speaking of self-hate, blacks leads in that category because they spend money on other ethnic groups rather than on their own people. Money in the black neighborhoods only go around once while other nationalities like Chinese and Caucasian money multiplies by 15 times before it leaves their neighborhoods. Thus, the reason there are hardly any black businesses.

Speaking of racism, that's something that will never go away and has always been here since God confused the language of men for trying to build a tower to reach the heavens. Racism is a disease or cancer that is converting humans into animals. Truthfully the only thing that can cure racism is interracial breeding. If all whites and blacks mate with only each other and the same goes for Indians and Chinese, it'll help cure racism. It may not be what God wanted but we're too ignorant to look beyond shades of color that we may need to blend in (Breed) the same color as our neighbor. Think about it, its 2014 and racism is still the ruler of this world or should I say in the most control of the configuration of this world. The police brutalities, the misjudge that sends innocent people to prison, the stereotypes, the ghettos, the BET, the hate crimes, is all a form of racism and the most racist people will debate against that. That's why I believe that the only way we can contain racism is to respect it and don't allow it to destroy us. Another fact is there are many racist people that don't even know they are until they get mad at the race different from them. Every nationality been a victim of racism but blacks and Jews suffered the most from it. Jews suffered because of Jesus was a Jew and also the Jews assassinated Jesus for blasphemy when Jesus claimed he was himself "God", and African Americans suffered because their skin color were darker shade. Yet many whites still try to put the blame on other Africans for selling their own people to slave owners which is not all that true. Whites went to their land and kidnapped them with forces of guns and nets. Knowing the fact the whites evidently couldn't communicate with the Indians so how could they negotiate so easy with Africans who spoke in a different tongue and had a different faith. And with all the gold and treasure they had in Africa, what were they trading their people for, boats? The truth is Africa used to be the richest country until it got stripped down for their wealth. America isn't ancient at all; it was built with the hands of other wealthy ancient countries. But maybe it was all God's plan for these things to happen because it sure was God's plan for the Israelites to sell themselves as slaves for food. So I am not complaining at all because I love America and I love all kinds of people even though they might not like my kind. But the point is that we're allowing ourselves to be defeated and ruled by racism. It's a proven fact because look at the separation of the shades of color around the world.

I want to merge self-hatred from racism in this paragraph, mainly to talk about African Americans, who are now feeding racism the most nutrients it needs to control this world. Yeah us black people are giving other racist people many reasons to stereotype us, misjudge us and think poorly of us. In order for us to overcome this self-hatred is to acknowledge what our black leaders has done for us. Even now when the most educated rapper like Loaded Lux speaks highly of Martin Luther King, Malcolm X or Huey Newton; he gets booed while his opponent glorifies sex, drugs and violence gets applauded. This shows you that we African Americans are taking steps back from what our African American leaders stepped forward for. Self-hatred: The straight hair wigs, the perms, the bleaching of the skin and the nose surgeries are all a form of self-hate. Perms have chemicals that destroy the hair follicles in cells which causes balding and then the reason for wigs. Yet African American women put this stuff in their daughter's hair so that she can look more of a Puerto Rican or White. What happen to black women looking black? What happen to being black and proud? What happen to the braids and afros? Black men were doing that in the 60s and 70s to be approved by whites and now black women are still doing it to be approved by both black and whites. Anything you're doing to be approved or accepted by someone has to be self-hate.

I always wanted to be a leader for the people that need the most help. Right now it's African Americans that have always been the people that needed the most help. The welfare, the EBT cards, the Obama care and all the other government handouts are shadowing our humanity for survival. It's nobody else fault but ours because we focus so much attention on our black celebrities that we forget that we have our own lives to live. To know all the lyrics to a rap song but never open up a book is why we're a laughing stock. To stand on line for 20 hours for a pair of 200 dollars pair of sneakers but don't have patience to go to college is one of the reasons many of us become homeless.

Our priorities are messed up because most black people follow a devilish trend and don't even know. Whatever is popular is what they follow because these kids act like they don't have a choice to listen to the music they want to because they're afraid of being laughed at, so they rather join the club of whatever is playing on the radio, (mostly sex). Why can't we all just write books instead of making videos about smoking and talking about girls' booty. Don't get me wrong I love my race I just hate the todays mentality of our race. Everything that Malcolm X and Dr. King fought for has gone to waste. But I never thought it was a good idea about King fighting for us to eat next to the whites because it became the reason we African Americans don't own any business today. You didn't see Chinese, Indians, Jamaicans or any other race begging to eat in someone else restaurants because they came together and built their own empire. So imagine if Dr. King and Malcolm had worked together. It wasn't the religious belief that separated them, it was the racist media. Just think about it we got thousands of Chinese restaurants, thousands of other foreign businesses but no African American businesses. Why? Because we cried to eat at a restaurant that didn't accept us and now we made their business successful. All the famous food restaurants you can think of were made very wealthy by mostly Afro Americans because they don't have their own. This is why they don't teach about Malcolm X in schools because they don't want us to identify ourselves. Malcolm X was trying to educate his people on who they are and tell them they were smart enough to have their own. Still blacks don't get it instead they rather beg the government to take care of them. Welfare and all the government assistance should only go to people who really need it, not people who are capable. And I also believe that if you have more kids than your financial strength, it shouldn't be the government responsibility to take care of what you couldn't. This is what imbalances the community and causes bigger debts. Not only African Americans failing to complete standard education, they're harden the situation by making multiple babies. I know this may seem like taking away someone's freedom but I believe if anyone can't take care of yourself you shouldn't be allowed to produce babies until you're financially stable.

Black leaders like Malcolm X fought all their life to restore our identity and now this generation wants to be proud of being a nigger. Being ignorant is becoming a new popular trend in the black community and when someone speaking knowledge he's looked at as a weirdo. Like the Holy Scriptures, history can never be outdated as it only clones itself because no one notices that they are repeating the past. People love to say "oh that's the past or it's been over" but the real fact is people are still modern slaves and racism still exists.

The point of this topic is that the 2k blacks are helping the New World Order to exist by the self-hate. As mostly the music industry are controlled by "Brainwashers" to badly influence the masses. The reason men today wear tighter jeans than their woman. Homosexuality is highly promoted and recommended in the music industry. History shows that the 60s and 70s blacks were becoming organized citizens but then the crack entered the black neighborhoods and destroyed what Malcolm X, Dr. King and the Black Panthers fought for. Now today the 2k blacks are reminding me of the 80s blacks because now everybody wants to get high. The Elites even used our president to legalize a drug favored by blacks just to keep them on the bottom. Any drug that kills your brain cells and lower your sperm cells and is legalized, is not legalized for your freedom to smoke it but to depopulate blacks. Just like the sugary drinks that's in every corner store are made to kill the sperm. Now ask yourself, what is the reason for "THEM" to put a chemical in a drink that kills sperm cells? And it's only selling in the black neighborhoods. This is part of the New World Order.

Chapter 5

Child Abuse

Child Abuse

Today, a parent can't register their children to go to school without getting poisonous injections. Those shots will usually make children get sick in the future when they're older, so that it can generate more money from man-made drugs. Those shots are so poisonous, that it kills blood cells year by year until the person gets very sick. It's like planting a virus in a computer until the computer doesn't work anymore. That's why it is best to give your child home schooling for the first 6 years of their life. The reason I call this child abuse because these poor innocent children are being treated like lab rats by being experimented on. Thus, the reason many children react differently on the drug dozes in them, and that's the reason we have many kids with cancer and other health problems. Today kids are developing more diseases and learning disabilities than 10-20 years ago; because the people who want to control the world want more money by selling incurable prescription drugs. Just like Christmas and Easter; this kind of child abuse is all a conspiracy to generate money; because why does a baby needs to be injected with so many shots as soon it is born? If you study the Holy Scriptures, no babies born were injected with needles and no diseases were known to newborns and no diseases were developed after. Now babies are injected with so many poisons that it causes diseases such as asthma, learning disabilities, organ problems and more. If the mother ate healthy and took care of herself while pregnant, how else did the baby come out full of diseases? The baby can't be cursed if he/she never lived before. The scriptures said "the sin of the parents will not affect the baby in the mother's stomach", meaning no new born should be punish due to their parents wrong doings. Another form of child abuse is parents who put make-up on their children. But we'll talk about that in the 10th chapter of this book. Meanwhile read more.

Today's most popular child abuse involve children in sex rings. Where wealthy organizations hold sex rings where adults can purchase children to have sex with them. Everyday a child goes missing and when they can't be located it is because they out of the country and sold off as a sex toy. Even some parents sell their kids for money or stage moms that sell their kids to Hollywood for acting/modelling jobs all for money. The most kids that get kidnap are the ones that travel by themselves. Parents that think their child is mature enough are totally wrong as the vulnerability of a lone child is very weak compared to a sex offender techniques. When most of the country is busy such as watching the Super Bowl or World Cup is when the sex trading is in the most effect. To lower the rate of missing children, parents need to step in and stop letting their 13 year old daughters go to the mall by themselves, keep eyes on them at the park, don't' let them travel by themselves (including getting on planes or trains) and avoid touring crowded cities like New York. Also never be late picking your child up from school as when anybody that looks like the child can get away with taking them home.

Another easy way a child can get snatch into a sex ring is when a child runs away from home. The biggest reason a child may run away from home is because of abuse whether it's physically or wordy. Parents think they are doing their child justice by beating them and showing it to the world like Facebook and WorldStar but really a child isn't learning anything from it but to have fear. Installing fear in a child for doing wrong is not the right discipline and will most likely backfire; as beating or whooping a child only gives them pain and pain is temporary. That child will say (wait til I'm 18 and I'm doing what I want) still all the beatings a child getting is only postponing his behavior until he/she is young adult. In fact, some kids will commit suicide when being abused like that from home. That's why it is better to have a full conversation on the subject focusing on the mistakes that child committed. That way a parent can educate the child on the things he/she did wrong. Yet parents expect a child to know better, but how can a child know better if their parents don't socialize with them. Some parents never mention sex or the importance of their child body to them, but as soon their child post naked pictures on a social network, the parents wants to beat their child brains out. Why? When the child never had anybody to talk to them about it; so therefore the parents are wrong, not the child. If the parents don't speak to their child about sex, and they go out and have sex, it's the parents fault not the child. So if parents want to discipline their child the right way they must use the most powerful weapon, the mouth.

Child abuse comes in many different forms other than physically abuse such as sexually abuse, wordy abuse, non-socializing abuse, same sex marriage (two adults of the same sex adopting a child) are all considered abuse. Especially gay couples adopting a child or faking a straight relationship with someone just to have a baby by them and then break up with them to keep custody of the child. I have seen many lesbian females use men to get them pregnant just because they like the way the men look and want their baby to look like him. It ends with a guy paying child support for a baby that he loses rights to. If a child doesn't grow up in the same household with both mother or father, it is child abuse. This is why it is safer to follow the Holy Scriptures rule of marriage; to get married before making babies and it also better to wait until you're at least 22 years and older. Having babies in your teen years and out of wedlock results most likely to divorce and break-ups. It is simple; if you don't plan on growing old with that person then don't have a baby by that person. The best way to secure a marriage is to first get baptized in the same religion, and then have babies. But people want to make babies with cute sexy people instead of people they want to grow old with. These last few generations prove that most women desire a cute baby instead of a long-term relationship, and most men wants a son but don't want to raise them. Men need to understand that a woman wanting to have a baby by him doesn't mean they truly love him or want to grow old with him. It's all about having baby showers and gaining popularity from a cute baby. Sadly this trend created a bunch of baby mamas and baby daddies. There are 20 percent more baby mamas and daddies than real marriage couples with kids living in the same household. 100 years ago the household was Father, Mother, Brother and Sister but now the household is Stepfather, Stepmom, Foster moms, Foster dad, Stepsisters and Stepbrothers. This means that there are not much real families left. Even I grew up in a household with a step father. Child abuse plays a huge role in the New World Order, as most pastors are already sexually abusing children for power and control.

Take Note: a lot of women use the child as a weapon for child support, a lot of men use "no job" as a shield for child support and again the child is the one who hurts....Every condom unworn should match the ring on the finger. If there's no ring on the finger, use that condom. That's real child support.

Chapter 6

Dealing with teens

Dealing with Teens

Teens are the easiest and most vulnerable targets for the people who want to slave the world. Today teens spend the most money on "New World Order" projects without even knowing. Teens urge to get out and be free but are slaving for the wicked "brainwashers". Today teens are the biggest promotion tools the brainwashers have. From video games, music, movies and internet; teens are trapped in the illusional media world that are using them to promote the New World Order. This wicked media makes them comfortable but at the same time brainwashing them. It makes them think they have the freedom to choose but the reverse phycology affects them very well in thinking they are free.

Dealing with teens today is a more difficult challenge than trying to make the Olympics team. Talking to them is like talking to a wall. Kids today are not the same as kids of yesterday (50 years ago). They have more freedom and exposure to the world more than any other kids of yesterday or ancient times. This much freedom is what makes them think they're grown. I had two human parents raising me but these kids are being raised by celebrities and electronic parents (internet). The internet is 90 percent junk, mostly porn and this is where most kids/teens are developing their personality from. Parents believe they are being fair by allowing these kids to live their life on the internet but really they are handicapping them. It would be okay if a child was using the social network to connect with family but the truth is they're not. The most popular social networks promote teen fights, child porn, homosexuality and everything else that will destroy the future of children.

Parents need to take back that parental position (being a boss) and show their kids true love and responsibility. Instead parents want to be their child best friend and that's the reason their kids will never respect them. Well maybe because most of these parents are still kids. You know the new trend these little girls follow; have a baby while in high school because it makes them popular. And a lot of these Television shows like "Teen Mom" and "16 and Pregnant" promote to these young girls that having a baby at a young age is a blessing and a gift. How is a single teen mom on welfare and nowhere to live is a gift from God? Some people are delusional. The fathers/baby daddies on "Teen Mom" is obviously young and full of ignorance with no job, forcing the situation to be more difficult. What did the 16 year old young pregnant teen thought? That the boy (baby's father) was going to take care of them like her father taking care of her mother? Education is beneficial and ignorance (lack of knowledge) is finding things out the hard way. Parents should go to talking to their kids about the Bible/Koran, about sex, about drugs, about money and everything else that a child will face one day. Not punishing your child for their wrong doings is crippling their mentality. Defending your child by saying "he didn't do it or she didn't do it knowing he/she did it is teaching your child to be irresponsible and will most likely become a prisoner. A child that is good at lying is a child that is bad at telling the truth; meaning no one will believe the child when he tells the truth. Even if it's something petty, a child should receive education on petty crimes that he/she committed or else the petty things he/she does will become a big issue one day. The hardest fact a parent has to deal with is that they know they can't keep an eye on their kids 24 hours because they're competing with school, other relatives, neighbors and the internet, which all can negatively influence your child. Every hour that you don't see your child could be the hour she/he is having sex, smoking, doing drugs, being molested, cursing, watching pornographic videos, fighting or any other bad things; but you know they're most likely not reading a book.

Chapter 7

Sexuality

Sexuality

Today sexuality changed rapidly from ten years ago to now. The increasing of dikes, transsexuals and homosexuality are numbering rapidly due to the influence of porn. The porn industry now has no limit to its morals. The most disgusting thing you can think of with sex; porn has displayed in every way possible. Today porn is promoting homosexuality more than straight porn. It is a known fact that porn is a major part of the "New World Order" and has been very successful by influencing millions of relationships to fail. It pretends to raise the bar of sex but it has successfully lowered the bar on human sexual morality; which ended millions of relationships. It creates a false desire and expectancy to which a couple always fails because they don't realize porn, especially TV porn is not real sex. I'm not sure but I remember one theory when a part of the New World Order was to turn everybody into homosexuals to balance the population. Whether true or not; that is the wrong path to manage the population of this world. I don't worry about the world being overcrowded because I believe the earth has a way of refreshing itself.

My thoughts on virginity

After a couple of religious scripture studies I gained much respect for a person's virginity. I wish I can take my virginity back until I get married so that I can lose it in the proper way. It was supposed to be a gift opened only by your married partner. Unfortunately I followed a popular trend in my teen years that it was so cool to have sex. Now I realize what I thought was cool is what creates hoes, hookers, unbalanced population, false relationships, low self-esteem in women, homosexuals, unwanted babies and regretful memories. Sure sex or receiving oral sex feels good but remember you're destroying a gift that was supposed to be opened by someone else. Think of virginity as a Christmas gift for someone. There was a precious gift for you under the tree but someone already opened your gift and when you receive your gift, it's already unwrapped and used. That's what I believe in a person's virginity that it should be saved for marriage and opened by his/her partner only because no one wants a used gift. This is why the divorce rate is so high because people gifts are already worn out. Even though it's too late for me because I have already lost my virginity, I hope that my future wife didn't lose hers but then it wouldn't be fair because I will be opening a new gift and she will be opening a used one. So I think it's fair to match used with used or marrying someone with the same sex experience. But I really don't want a woman

that has been shared and exposed before. I
want to open a new gift.

Homosexuality

Many people confuse homosexuality
as a natural lifestyle. It is instead a
rebellious form of separation or being
different supported by "brainwashers". No
child is born homosexual or grows up
homosexual until his/her mind is influenced
to rebel against human natural orders. How
does a child becomes homosexual? There
are many ways a person chooses that
lifestyle and some became that way by being
molested, rape, same sex parents and
influenced by television. Especially today,
homosexuality is promoted everywhere
possible. Even doctors today report trying to
infuse female hormones or DNA inside of
males to produce natural homosexuals and
vice versa. Every mother that delivers a

baby should keep watch of their baby at all times. When doctors or nurses take the baby into another room, the parents should follow. The doctors may claim that they need privacy to run a test, but to your ignorance they might be running an experiment. Just like doctors in the 70s going to African countries claiming they're healing the sick but they were actually spreading the AIDS virus to African patients by sticking infected needles claiming it to be antibiotics. Yes, doctors were ordered to wipe out Africa with their deceiving medical supplies. That's why many people in Africa were dying from AIDS at one time. But we'll get into that in the next chapter.

For women, the lesbian thing is fake like flying pigs. If lesbians are real then how come lesbians use dildos (fake penises) for sexual pleasure or stick anything penis-like into their vaginas? It's like taking only the sexual part of man and disowning the rest and considering themselves lesbians. I believe a lesbian should enjoy the woman body parts only. There's nothing you should like about a man if you're a lesbian. And another fact that makes me believe that lesbianism is fraud is the one that looks like a woman dates dikes (the one that looks like a man). If lesbian means girl liking girl then she can't be considered a lesbian if she's like a dike (a woman who pretends to be a man). It just doesn't make since. You can't be homosexual if you like someone that looks and act like the opposite sex. A real lesbian is a woman who likes another woman that dress, act and looks like a woman. Luckily I never saw a real lesbian before. This is why I believe homosexuality is a form of rebellion, a way of acting out in hopes someone come along and changes them. Sadly some people will say "Well there are homosexualities in animals". Well we are humans not animals. In fact, most of the animals these people are talking about are breeded; not God's creations. Take Note: Human being means to be capable of God's qualities. And the scriptures never said animals were capable of God's qualities...The bible says look at the beasts (animals), that they will teach us. That don't mean we should act like animals. The brainwashers are trying to change our sexuality to reduce human nature and to control us.

Where did the AIDS virus come from?

Debunking the "Out of Africa" Origin of
HIV & AIDS
The Greatest Conspiracy Story Ever Told
By Alan Cantwell, M.D.

*AIDS is now more than a quarter-century
old. The disease has killed
20 million people worldwide, and it is
estimated that 40 million more
are infected with HIV, the virus that causes
AIDS.*

*Most physicians will probably the epidemic
of AIDS started when monkeys or chimps in
the African bush transferred the AIDS virus
(HIV) to a person while butchering
primate meat for food or through an animal
bite. For the first two
decades of the epidemic the green monkey
theory of AIDS was widely
heralded in the major media, and was
accepted without question by
leading AIDS experts and educators. The
theory was so universally
popular (except in Africa) that it easily*

became fact in the minds of most people.

Robert Gallo, M.D., and the Green Monkey Theory

The AIDS virus was first discovered by Robert Gallo at the National Cancer Institute in April 1984. Shortly thereafter Luc Montagnier of the Pasteur Institute in Paris claimed that he (and not Gallo) had first discovered the AIDS virus. A bitter lawsuit followed, which was finally settled privately in 1987 through the intervention of the French Premier and President Ronald Reagan. To this day, the two 'co-discoverers' of HIV continue to disagree about the origin of HIV and the birthplace of AIDS.

In Montagnier's book, Virus (2000), he states: "The origin of the epidemic remains a mystery, and the virus seems older than the epidemic" and "it is important to distinguish between the origins of the virus and that of the (AIDS) epidemic."

The scientific scandal provoked by Gallo's "stealing" the virus from the French, as well as the ensuing government investigations into allegations of scientific irregularities and falsification of data in Gallo's lab, undoubtedly is the reason both scientists have never received a Nobel Prize for their discovery of HIV. A highly unsympathetic account of this scientific mess is provided by Pulitzer prize-winning author John Crewdson in, Science Fictions; A Scientific Mystery, A Massive Cover-Up, and the Dark Legacy of Robert Gallo (2002).

Because Gallo is the most powerful and influential AIDS scientist, his views on the origin of HIV/AIDS have become gospel. He first called his AIDS virus the "human T-cell leukemia/lymphoma virus" because he believed it was closely related to

newly discovered
cancer-causing retroviruses. The virus was
quickly renamed human
T-cell lymphotropic virus-3 (HTLV-3),
perhaps to obscure the
connection of the AIDS virus to laboratory
cancer viruses, and to
downplay any association between cancer
(which is thought to be
non-contagious) and AIDS (which is
definitely a sexually-transmitted
disease).

Robert Gallo, M.D. says AIDS is an
epidemic of cancer. In the 1970s
the knowledge achieved by the study of
cancer
retroviruses helped lead to the discovery of
the
AIDS virus in 1984. Unfortunately, the
presence
of "cancer microbes" in cancer and AIDS
has been
totally ignored by the medical establishment.

Where did Gallo's new virus come from? In
the prestigious journal

Science (Jan 4, 1985) it was reported that Gallo's AIDS virus was most closely related to "slow viruses" (lentiviruses) found in sheep and goats, particularly the visna virus in sheep, which causes pneumonia, neurologic changes, and wasting. However, Gallo declared that his virus was not visna virus, but might be "another animal viruses coming into man...and this means we have to look more closely at these animals as models and these types of animal viruses. No one knows if the viruses could have stemmed from a common viral ancestor hundreds or thousands of years ago, or if a virus moved between species only decades ago from human exposure to the virus of sheep or goats."

The idea that HIV was "closely related" to the sheep visna virus did not last long. The idea of a sheep virus infecting gay men would have undoubtedly aroused suspicion because the

only place one could find
visna was in research labs where visna virus
had been seeded and
"adapted" into various animal species, as
well as into human cells,
for the two decades prior to the "gay
plague."

Gallo, with the help of veterinarian Max
Essex of Harvard, convinced
the AIDS experts and the adoring media that
AIDS came from green
monkeys. In Gallo's book *Virus Hunting*
[1991], he claims that in 1983
(a year before his discovery) Ann Giudici
Fettner, a free-lance
journalist who had lived in Africa, told him
that the virus came from
green monkeys in central Africa. In 1983 the
African connection to
AIDS was tenuous, and in Fettner's 1984
book, *The Truth About AIDS,*
she never mentioned green monkeys and the
African origin of AIDS. In
fact, on page 44, she emphatically states:
"AIDS started as an
American disease."

There are no scientific papers which uphold
the green monkey theory.
The monkey out of Africa theory lasted until
the late 1990s when
another group of American scientists
claimed the virus definitely
originated in a specific species of
chimpanzee found in Africa.

The green monkey theory was scientifically
doomed from the very
start, although that apparently did not phase
the scientists who
undoubtedly wanted to place the blame on
the dark continent -- and
take the origin of HIV out of Manhattan,
where the first cases were
discovered in 1979, and push the origin to
the other side of the
world.

*The Marriage of Cancer Research and
Biowarfare in 1971*

*Whatever the theoretical origin of
HIV/AIDS, there is no doubt that
the epidemic started a decade after scientists
began "adapting"
massive numbers of cancer-causing and
immunosuppressive animal
viruses and transferring them between
various animal species in an
attempt to experimentally produce cancer in
the laboratory. In the
process of these "species-jumping"
experiments, the scientists mixed
viruses together, seeded them into the bodies
of various animal
species, and planted them into animal and
human cell cultures. In the
process myriads of new, laboratory-created
mutant, hybrid and
recombinant viruses were created, some of
which were exceedingly
dangerous.*

*These engineered and deadly viruses were
obviously of interest to
biowarfare scientists. Donald A MacArthur
stated in Congressional
testimony in 1969 that "molecular biology is
a field that is
advancing very rapidly and eminent
biologists believe that within a
period of 5 to 10 years it would be possible
to produce a synthetic
biological agent, an agent that does not exist
naturally exist and
for which no natural immunity could have
been acquired."*

*The dangers provoked by all these
laboratory-created new virus were
well known. At a symposium on leukemia
research in 1973, Danish
pathologist J Clemmesen warned that the
transmissibility of these
genetically -altered viral agents could cause
a world epidemic of
cancer if they escaped from the laboratory.
(Gallo has publicly
stated AIDS is an epidemic of cancer.) That
same year cancer*

virologists convened at a conference entitled "Biohazards in
Biological Research" at Asilomar, California. Despite the risks, it
was decided to continue perilous animal cancer virus experimentation.

People are often surprised to find there is a close relationship
between traditional cancer virus research and biological warfare
programs and experimentation. However, it is a fact that in 1971
President Richard Nixon, as part of his War On Cancer, combined the
U.S. Army's biowarfare department at Ft. Detrick, Maryland, with the
National Cancer Institute. The army's DNA and genetic engineering
programs were coordinated into anti-cancer research and molecular
biology programs. This marriage also cemented the governmental ties
of cancer research to the CIA, the CDC, the World Health
Organization, and private industry.

During this same period the Special Virus Cancer Program (1968-1980),
now largely and conveniently forgotten, was established to coordinate
the search for cancer-causing viruses. The U.S. biological warfare
program is highly secret. This secrecy also surrounds the many
scientists who directly or indirectly contribute to the program.
Naturally, there is no complete record of what this Virus Cancer
Program has achieved or what cancer-causing and immunosuppressive
animal cancer viruses were adapted for biological warfare use and for
covert military testing on human populations. For more details type-in key words :
biological warfare human experimentation.)

A computer PUBMED search employing the key words "U.S. Army
Biological Warfare Program" yields only 44 citations. One entry
(PMID: 11572136) reads: "The United States began its BW program based

on intelligence information and a very thorough evaluation of that information by a panel of scientists, engineers, medical personnel from a variety of areas including the military, other government agencies, industry, and the academic community. Initial efforts were directed toward defense against BW, but it soon became clear defense required a knowledge of offensive capabilities. The initial offensive studies started with a definition of what infectious organisms were available, how they could grow in quantities to support a munitions program, what kind of facilities were required, and where they could be positioned. Further studies were then initiated to design and evaluate testing sites and methodologies to evaluate the weapons. During all of these phases, concurrent medical and safety programs were studied, emphasized, and implemented. These studies resulted in the development of a number of vaccines,

toxoids, treatments,
therapies, and facility personnel
management. The overall conclusion
was that BW, offensive and defensive, was
possible, and efficiencies
could be obtained. The work accomplished
by this group of very
dedicated military and civilian personnel at
military installations,
universities, research institutes, and
industrial organizations
presented truly a combined operation with
numerous achievements. Many
of the detailed achievements were published
in the open scientific,
peer-reviewed journals, and many patents
were obtained. The current
defensive program is breaking new scientific
ground and there is
evidence indicating that very rapid detection
and identification of
BW agents is possible and will be
instrumented."

Is it "conspiracy theory" to question whether
a virus "closely
related" to HIV was created in any of the

many laboratories
contributing to the Special Virus Cancer
Program and its connection
to biowarfare research during the 1970s?
Could covert human testing
of classified biowarfare agents explain the
exclusive "introduction"
of HIV into gay men, the most hated
minority in America, via the
government-sponsored experimental
hepatitis B experiments that began
in Manhattan in New York City in 1978 --
the year before the onset of
the "gay plague."

The American Origin of AIDS in 1979

In 1979 the first young white gay men to
come down with "gay-related
immunodeficiency disease" was reported to
the CDC. For the first year
of the epidemic all the men were from
Manhattan. They were all
defined as young, predominantly white,
previously healthy,
well-educated and promiscuous.

*The Manhattan men were similar in profile
to the 1,083 gay men who
signed up for the hepatitis B experiment
conducted at the New York
Blood Center, also located in Manhattan.
The experimental vaccine was
developed in chimpanzees. The injections
began in November 1978, and
were concluded a year later. Similar vaccine
experiments in gay men
were undertaken in San Francisco, Los
Angeles, Denver, St. Louis and
Chicago, beginning in March 1980 and
continued until October 1981, a
few months after the epidemic had become
"official"*

*AIDS became official in the U.S. in June
1981. At the time AIDS was
unknown in Africa, and the epidemic did not
begin there until autumn
1982 at the earliest. After Gallo discovered
HIV in April 1984, an
HIV blood test was developed and was used
on the stored gay blood
specimens deposited at the Center as part of
the ongoing experiment*

and follow-up. In 1980, a year before the
epidemic became official,
already 20% of the men's blood in the
experiment were HIV-positive.
By 1983, 30% of the men were positive; by
1984, 40%.

AIDS scientists repeatedly claim HIV was
lurking in Africa for
decades, centuries, even millennia, before
the epidemic. But there
was no "incubation period" in America.

As soon as large numbers of gay people
came out of the closet and
signed up for government experiments, the
gay community was doomed.
Not only was one virus (HIV) "introduced"
into the homosexual
population, but two additional
"mycoplasma" bacteria-like agents and
a new herpes virus as well. In addition, I
wrote in books and medical
journals that "cancer-causing bacteria"
were also operative in AIDS,
but all my research linking AIDS to cancer
remains ignored by the

AIDS establishment.

"Gay Cancer": A mystery wrapped in an enigma

Three years before HIV was discovered, my research uncovering
bacteria in Kaposi's sarcoma was published. KS became widely known as
the "gay cancer" associated with AIDS. In the late 1970s, as a
dermatologist, I studied the cancerous tissue of three elderly,
presumably straight married men with KS, a very rare skin cancer that
few physicians had ever seen. I identified bacteria in the cancerous
tissue; and bacteria were cultured from skin biopsies. When the first
gay men with KS appeared in my office, I studied their skin tumors
for bacteria. A PUBMED computer search lists 7 of my research papers
published in medical journals between the years 1981-1986 showing
bacteria in the KS lesions of straight and gay men with KS and AIDS,

in the enlarged lymph nodes of "AIDS-
related complex", and in two
autopsy studies showing bacteria in the
internal organs of a straight
man who died of KS before the epidemic,
and a gay man who died of KS
and AIDS.

My bacterial research showed a close
relationship of AIDS to
cancer. This research is included in my
books, AIDS:The
Mystery & the Solution (1984), and The
Cancer Microbe (1990). When
Gallo was asked about my KS research in a
published interview by
James D'Eramo in 1984, he ignored the
question. When asked why only
homosexuals were the first victims of AIDS,
he replied: "Because they
were exposed." To this day Gallo and
Montagnier refuse to acknowledge
any aspect of this research.

In 1993, Shyh-Ching Lo of the Armed
Forces Institute of Pathology
reported the finding of 2 different infectious

agents in the blood,
urine and KS tumors of AIDS patients. At
first, he thought the
microbes were viruses, but later determined
they were actually very
small forms of bacteria called
"mycoplasmas." After Lo's discovery,
the Army quickly took out patents on his
infectious agents, which he
calls Mycoplasma fermentens and M.
penetrans. My KS research was
never mentioned in any of his papers.

In 1994, a new infectious and sexually-
transmitted herpes virus
called "human herpes virus-8" was
proclaimed to be the agent causing
all pre-AIDS and AIDS-related KS. This
virus is now widely accepted
as the sole cause. I thought it rather strange
that there was never
any evidence that KS was transmissible
before AIDS, and that a "new"
virus could cause a rare cancerous disease
that has been around since
the 1870s.

Montagnier thinks mycoplasmas might be a
necessary "co-factor" which
accelerates the progression of HIV infection
in AIDS patients. He
also believes antibiotic therapy along with
antiviral therapy is
better treatment for AIDS. Where did these
new mycoplasmas come from?
Where did HIV come from? Offering
homophobic explanations and no
evidence in his Virus book, the French
virologist theorizes that
American gay tourists brought back these
agents from Africa to the
U.S.

Evidence of blood infection with the new KS
human herpes virus-8 is
now present in as many as 40% of men with
prostate cancer. In Texas,
15% of normal blood donors now test
positive for the virus. This
means the virus is in the American blood
supply; and blood is not
screened for the virus. Where did the "new"
herpes virus come from? A
"close relative" is the Herpes saimiri virus

of squirrel monkeys, a
virus that was extensively passed around in
the Special Virus Cancer
Program.

Chimpanzees and the Polio Vaccine Theory
of AIDS

In 1999 the publication of The River: A
Journey to the Source
of HIV and AIDS, by journalist Edward
Hooper, received
widespread media attention. Hooper
theorizes that HIV was introduced
into Africans via chimp virus-contaminated
polio vaccine programs in
the late 1950s. His massive book does not
adequately explain why it
took 30 years for the epidemic to appear in
Africa, nor how a
sexually-transmitted disease in black
Africans in the early 1980s
could have transformed itself into a white
gay man's disease in New
York City in the late 1970s. Furthermore,
there are no HIV-positive
tissue or blood specimens from Africa from

76

the 1960s and 1970s, and
no proven cases of AIDS either, to indicate HIV was "incubating" in
the African population. Hooper quickly dismisses the claims of Robert
Strecker, the first physician whistle-blower of man-made AIDS, as
well as the man-made research in my own two books on the man-made
origin: *AIDS & The Doctors of Death,* and *Queer Blood.*

By predating his polio vaccine theory back to the late 1950s, Hooper
greatly simplified his theory of AIDS origin. He ignores all the
primate/simian viruses that were placed into human tissue in the 60s
and 70s, and all those genetically altered viruses for cancer
research, vaccine research, and secret biological warfare.

The chimp in the freezer at Fort Detrick
On February 1, 1999 Lawrence K Altman, M.D, longtime AIDS-writer for
The New York Times, dutifully reported "the

riddle of the origin of
the AIDS virus has apparently been solved."
A team of researchers,
headed by Beatrice Hahn at the University
of Alabama, performed viral
studies on three chimps in the African wild
and studied the frozen
remains of a chimp, discovered by accident
in a freezer at the Army's
biowarfare center at Fort Detrick. The
chimp had tested positive for
HIV in 1985. On the basis of this research,
Hahn declared that a
common subspecies of chimp (Pan
troglodytes troglodytes) was the
animal source of the virus "most closely"
related to HIV. In a media
blitz U.S. government scientists presented a
phylogenetic ancestral
"family tree" of primate viruses (which few
people could understand)
to prove that HIV was genetically descended
from a chimp virus in the
African bush.
Hahn theorizes the epidemic could have
started when a hunter became
infected by cutting himself while butchering

*chimp meat. Back in the
1980s Hahn worked in Gallo's lab, and like
Gallo she ignores the
entire history of animal cancer virus
laboratory transfers in the
decades preceding AIDS, as well as the fact
that chimp kidneys were
transplanted into humans back in the 1960s
in New York City. Another
big problem is that after scientists pump
viruses into captive lab
chimps in laboratories in the U.S. and
Africa, they sometimes release
them back into the wild. Obviously, the mix
of lab animal viruses
with viruses in the wild make the
determination of viral "ancestry"
somewhat iffy.*

*AIDS scientists totally accepted Hahn's
notion that HIV jumped
species from chimps to humans back in the
1930s to start the
epidemic. The media again explained this
was the first time that
primate viruses had jumped species
"naturally," again failing to*

*mention all the millions of people around
the world who had the
primate/simian SV40 virus injected into
them along with their polio
shot.*

*How accurate and meaningful is the
ancestry of all these animal
retroviruses? Do words used by scientists to
compare different
viruses, such as "closely related" and
"distally related" (meaning
related far from the point of origin) really
tell us how a suspected
primate virus like HIV got into the human
population? For example, it
is widely reported in scientific circles that
no two HIV viruses are
exactly alike. This is because HIV mutates
readily and takes on some
of the molecular components of the cells it
invades. When it comes to
viral "relationships" the only absolutely
identical HIV viruses in
scientific history was the virus presented by
Gallo as his discovery,
and the virus presented by Montagnier as*

his discovery. The genetic
evidence indicated it was impossible for
these two scientists to have
discovered identical viruses on two different
continents, even though
Gallo insisted his virus was not the same as
Montagnier's. Thus, the
lawsuit.
The moral of this story is: If the two most
highly respected AIDS
scientists cannot agree on the ancestry of
identical twin viruses,
then how can we be sure when they tell us
which virus is related to
which virus -- particularly when many
engineered laboratory viruses
are not even recorded and entered into so-
called virus banks or
registries which are used to compare the
genetic make-up of "known"
viruses. Let's face it, if your old ancestors
are not recorded in a
book somewhere, you will never find them as
ancestors.

The Origin of AIDS Conference, London,
2000

In October 2000 the Royal Society of
London held a two-day conference
on the origins of HIV. Needless to say, the
man-made theory was not
discussed. One professor emphatically
declared: "All human infectious
diseases have an animal origin." Hooper's
polio theory was totally
discredited; and Hahn's new chimp theory,
dating HIV back to the
1930s, was acclaimed.

The "Last Word" at the conference was that
"all human viral
infections were initially zoonotic (animal) in
origin. Animals will
always provide a reservoir for viruses that
could threaten human
populations in the future." The scientists
predicted: "There is still
a myriad of current unknown viruses in
animal populations on land,
sea, and air with the potential to cause
human disease." But what

about the millions of dangerous virus
created in animal laboratories?
That was never considered.

A person cannot contract AIDS from a
monkey or chimp

In the July 2000 issue of Lancet, virologist
and primatologist
Preston Marx states: "There is no evidence
that a person can contract
AIDS from a monkey or chimpanzee".
According to Marx, research shows
humans were infected with SIV (simian
immunodeficiency virus) in
Africa and that these SIV infections were the
root origin of HIV.
Therefore SIV is the monkey ancestor virus
of HIV. And Marx has no
doubt that HIV originated from SIV in
African non-human primates.

AIDS educators often claim that AIDS is a
"zoonosis", meaning a
disease of animals that can be transmitted to
humans, but Marx says
this assumption is incorrect. AIDS as a

*zoonosis would mean that
humans had contracted not only an SIV
infection from a monkey or a
chimp, but that they also eventually became
sick with AIDS from the
monkey virus infection. We have not
established that AIDS is a
zoonosis (meaning a disease people catch
from monkeys). He further
declares "We do not know what launches
animal viruses to become
epidemic in humans. There may be a social,
viral-genetic or
immunologic basis for new epidemics. We
do not have this answer for
the AIDS epidemic, but we do know that HIV
originated from simian
species."*

*In a more recent October 2004 article
"AIDS as a zoonosis? Confusion
over the origin of the virus and the origin of
the epidemic", Marx
and his colleagues further speculate that
HIV (derived from a
primate) in the 1950s in Africa could have
been made more dangerous*

and transmissible by dirty needles used in vaccine programs, as well
as contaminated blood transfusions. The repeated passage from
human-to-human (so called "serial passage") via SIV
virus-contaminated needles could have transformed a harmless SIV in
humans to the deadly and genetically-changed HIV virus causing AIDS.

Human exposure to SIV is thousands of years old, but AIDS merged only
in the 20th century. Marx never suggests that contaminated vaccines,
rather than needles, could have initiated the African epidemic.
However, if AIDS does not qualify as a zoonosis, I interpret this to
mean that Hahn's "cut hunter theory" could not account for the
explosion of HIV/AIDS in Africa in the 1980s. Finally, Marx's team
suggests that more "research is needed to understand the processes by
which animal viruses cause sustained human-to-human transmission,

*epidemics and even pandemics. Much is
known about emerging viruses,
but almost nothing is known about emerging
viral diseases."*

WHO Murdered Africa?

*Apparently forgotten, ignored, or unknown
by Marx was a similar
vaccine and needle scenario reported on
May 11, 1987, on the
front-page of The London Times, entitled
"Smallpox vaccine triggered
AIDS virus." Science editor Pierce Wright
suggested that African AIDS
was a direct result of the World Health
Organization's smallpox
eradication program conducted in the
1970s. The smallpox vaccine
allegedly awakened a "dormant" AIDS virus
infection in the black
population. Gallo was quoted as saying,
"The link between the WHO
program and the epidemic is an interesting
and important hypothesis.
I cannot say that it actually happened, but I
have been saying for*

some years that the use of live vaccines such as that used for
smallpox can activate a dormant infection such as HIV (the AIDS
virus)."

The Times report is one of the most important stories ever printed on
the AIDS epidemic; yet the story was killed and never appeared in any
major U.S. newspaper or magazine. However, the report is widely
circulated on the internet as evidence to suggest that AIDS appeared
in Africa via accidental or deliberate vaccine contamination with the
AIDS virus. (Google: WHO murdered Africa).

Kenyan ecologist and biologist Wangari Maathai was obviously aware of
this vaccine connection when she won the Nobel Peace Prize in October
2004, and shocked reporters by claiming the AIDS virus was a
deliberately created biological agent developed by evil-minded

*scientists and released in Africa to cause
mass extermination of
blacks.*

*In Magic Shots [1982], Allan Chase claims
that during the years
1966-1977, the WHO utilized "200,000
people in forty countries --
most of them non-doctors trained by seven
hundred doctors and health
professionals from over seventy
participating countries -- spent $300
million, and used forty million bifurcated
vaccinating needles to
administer 24,000 million (2.4 billion) doses
of smallpox vaccine."
This is also proof of extensive needle re-use.*

*There is absolutely no evidence to show that
large numbers of African
blacks were "incubating" HIV, or any other
primate/simian virus
before the outbreak. This is why the out of
Africa idea is theory and
not fact.*

Despite this lack of evidence, the monkey/chimp and primate/simian origin of HIV/AIDS is a well-accepted scientific theory. In contrast, the man-made "introduction" of HIV in the late 1970s is condemned as "conspiracy theory". Although taboo, the man-made theory refuses to go away, and is alive and well on the internet. A google search, using the key words "man made origin of AIDS," will elicit 1,220,000 citations to various web sites.

HIV: Out of Africa? Or out of a virus laboratory?

Precise answers to how AIDS originated depends on which "expert" you ask. Montagnier points to the United States and gay men as the source of the virus. Could the virus have been transmitted from chimpanzees to humans? Montagnier says yes. But, he adds, humans could have transmitted the virus to the chimpanzees! How could humans have

transmitted the virus to chimps?
Unfortunately, the Frenchman did not
elaborate on this.

Could HIV be a primate/simian virus
originating in a virus laboratory
? Such questions are never seriously
proposed or answered by
virologists. However, well-known to insiders
are the embarrassing
contamination problems with primate
viruses which have plagued
Gallo's lab at the NCI and Essex's lab at
Harvard.

A case in point is Gallo's reported 1975
"discovery" of a "new" and
"human" virus reported in scientific journals
as "HL-23." This virus
was eventually proven to be not one, but
three different ape viruses
(gibbon-ape virus, simian sarcoma virus and
baboon endogenous virus).
Gallo claims he has no idea how these
viruses contaminated his
research.

*Essex, who along with Gallo heavily
promoted the erroneous green
monkey theory, had similar woes. In 1986 he
announced the discovery
of a "new" human AIDS virus (HTLV-4).
This "human" virus bore a
striking similarity to a monkey retrovirus
known as STLV-3. In
February 1988, the mystery was solved.
Essex's new "human" HTLV-4
virus turned out to be a monkey virus that
accidentally contaminated
Essex's human blood samples. The source of
the monkey contamination
was traced back to blood samples from a
monkey that was
experimentally infected by an AIDS-like
virus at the New England
Regional Primate Research Center in
Southborough, Massachusetts.
Carol Mulder of the University of
Massachusetts Medical School
cautioned: "This episode should serve as a
strong warning for all
virologists to check any newly discovered
viruses against viruses
present in the laboratory."*

*In the decade before AIDS broke out in gay
men, Essex created "cat
AIDS" in a series of experiments. In 1974,
chimpanzee AIDS was also
created deliberately by feeding heavily
virus-contaminated cows' milk
to newborn chimps. For the very first time,
veterinarians were able
to produce leukemia in chimps, as well as a
lung infection, later
known as the "gay pneumonia" of AIDS. As
Montagnier should be aware,
human cancerous tissue and blood was
routinely injected into primates
as part of the Special Virus Cancer
Program. Mysterious AIDS-like
illnesses also occurred in primate
laboratories a few years before
AIDS. And chimp viruses also jumped
species back in the 1960s when
chimp kidneys were experimentally
transplanted into humans.*

*We are informed that the AIDS epidemic is
the result of a primate
virus jumping species for the first time.
However, polio vaccines*

given to millions of people in the 50s and 60s were heavily
contaminated with a cancer-causing monkey virus called SV-40 (simian
virus 40). Over the decades various studies indicate this virus is
implicated in several forms of human cancer, although government
scientists continue to deny any association.

The man-made theory of AIDS proclaims that HIV was introduced into
American gays and African blacks via vaccine programs. Why is this
theory deemed paranoia by the media and the AIDS establishment? Why
is this discussion not allowed? Why have scientists suppressed the
extensive history of animal cancer virus transfer in the decade
before AIDS?

Is there a scientific conspiracy to get scientists off the hook by
blaming monkeys in the bush, and gays and Africans, for the millions
of death brought about by the "introduction"

of HIV into the world
population? Of course there is. That's why
it's The Greatest
Conspiracy Story Ever Told.

What I learned from this story is never get vaccinated. I always knew vaccines were a fluke as I notice people who take it gets sicker.

Chapter 8

Smoking

Smoking

The Elites wants half of the population to smoke itself to death. Whatever type of smoking a person does is damaging their lungs. Though cigarettes smoke has thousands of harmful cancerous chemicals; however it is still legal to smoke. Why, because it kills people which make room for other people and it is used to collect millions of tax money. Getting rid of cigarettes will cause tax problems. Though weed is more beneficial than cigarettes, the reason it is illegal because it is a threat to the health organization. Though smoking too much of it is harmful to your health. But America has to sacrifice millions of lives in order to stay on top of the wealth race. Cigarettes are a big factor to this country, it makes room and it pays bills.

I never understood why people smoke cigarettes or why do the Government allow it to be sold to be smoked. But for some reason weed aka marijuana is illegal to smoke which is less cancerous than tobacco according to the current information we have. Marijuana makes you high and tobacco makes you calm but both of the drugs have its own share of side effects. Weed may have same amount of beneficial effects as dangerous effects. The reason weed is illegal in most states is because it will affect the profit of the organizations that supposedly support our health. It's all a conspiracy to keep money flowing to provide for their businesses. Ever saw the TV commercials for these over the counter drugs that have the same side effects as the last drug that got removed. It is the same drug but with a different name; the purpose is to continue the sacrifices. There are

natural cures for your sickness but they
rather lead you with scams as long as they
can so they can profit. 90 percent of the
health organizations profit off of sacrifices
(drug testing on people). Any drug that you
buy that has been commercialized, you
become their test subject. It's the same thing
when they feed mice chemicals to see how it
reacts. So they give these prescription pills
to us and if more people survive from the
drug than die, they'll keep it on the shelf
longer. When the pill hit the set number of
deaths that it caused, they remove it quick as
possible before it becomes major news so
that people don't see the health
organizations for what it really is, greedy.
They sell you a drug "xxx" then when you
get sick they sell you another drug just about
as bad as the "xxx", and tell you this will
cure the sickness what the "xxx" caused.
Back to cigarettes, I don't smoke it and

never will; for a reason that it destroyed my family. My stepfather saw that it was unattractive for my mother to smoke so it helped him to make a decision to a divorce. My mother developed lung cancer which she is currently on a machine to assist her in breathing. I lost a few cousins and an aunt due to smoking; therefore I have my reasons not to smoke. I always thought if people want to kill themselves why they don't just jump off a roof or put a gun to their head and ended quickly. At least you don't have to go through years of struggling to breathe, walk or get out of bed. Nothing worse than dying slow so don't smoke cigarettes, there are cooler ways to die.

Chapter 9

Secrets of Cheaters/Can Women and Men be friends

Pre introduction

We all sinfully cheaters but we can be forgiven

Love don't cost a thing but we make it expensive

If we take our women for granted, someone will come along and appreciate what we didn't

Females don't want some attention they want all of the attention

A jealous girlfriend is a caring girlfriend

Women are meant to be loved not understood but its pleasure to them if they see us listen

If your man says yes to everything, he is not listening

*Being a leader is being lonely, so both
should make the decisions*

*A perfect marriage is one who marries their
best friend*

*A relationship is friendship, caring, trust
and happiness*

*If your relationship involves stress, anger,
attitude and other negative feelings, then
you're not in a relationship you're in prison*

*Every moment should be more memorized
than a flood*

*Because time converts hours into hardwired
love*

*That'll make your relationship end with a
happy ending*

*Spending time improves the all-around
quality because love is indefinite*

*A clean house is a happy home meanwhile a
dirty house signifies the relationship is
pretending*

*Learn to give space because fresh air keeps
it spinning*

*Flirting helps you stay sexually active and
keeps your sex drive relevant*

Laughing kills all the worries and enhance the french

Boredom can paralyzed the relationship so try new things to stabilize the interest

Unexpected gifts puts on the biggest smiles and it don't have to be expensive

So no matter who's cheating, praying helps and heals the negative feelings

Introduction

I am not an expert in relationship but my past experience makes me an expert in the decisions I make today. In fact I don't think anyone is because woman are the second most complicated living thing next to the human brain; and men "simplicity" makes the relationships even more complicated. I am no expert but from my research, my curiosity, and my experiences of studying couples; gave me enough information and education to influence readers of this chapter to improve their relationships. I am sure to be 99% sure that you'll love the solution I give you to your problems because my answers are base off biblical knowledge, higher learning and personal experiences. This chapter is intended to improve your relationship and cure the cheater disease we all sinfully contain.

Cheaters

What is a cheater? Cheaters (male and female) are the ones that have sexual or mental intercourse outside the marriage or relationship.

I have been in long-term and short term relationships and each relationship ended in someone cheating. So after researching my past relationships and friends and family relationships, I discovered that everybody is pretty much a cheater, well at least everybody that I know. But anyway I am going to tell you some stories from my experience in hopes to shape up your own relationships and even your thoughts.

Well I am single today because me and my ex wasn't the perfect match, or should I say her perfect match. Our relationship failed not because someone cheated, it was because I was too nice. I grew up in a house full of girls and I loved my sisters and mother dearly, so I treated woman how I would treat my sisters. But one thing I didn't know is that "too nice" guys are a turn off for 95% of woman in this country. It's funny that a person like me grows up in a house full of girls and we're taught not to hit girls back and treat your mom like a queen. Why, nobody ever told me that I will have to treat woman the opposite when I get a girlfriend if I wanted to maintain the relationship. Well since the experiences, I decided that I'm going to stay my "nice guy ways" and not change for anybody because I believe out of 150 million of females in this country, there got to be at least one that will appreciate my "nice guy" ways. Truthfully I never understood why most females fear when a guy is being nice to them. It shames me that when a guy cleans up, cooks for his wife, wash his own clothes; that he seem weak to the female, this is why I believe that American woman are like robots because they allow themselves to be brainwashed by some weird society. According to society standards, nice guys finish last because females are brainwashed believing good guys aren't confident and bad guys are confident. Really it's the good guys who are secure and the bad guys who are insecure, which is the reason they don't respect them and treat them bad. Most women don't know what they want and allow their mind to play tricks on them.

In America, no women or men will ever find their true soul mate because America has brainwashed people to see only material things as beautiful and positive. The new era of women wants to find a man with celebrity status or qualities, or someone that looks like a famous person. This is why America has one of the highest divorce rates in the world because many people marry for the wrong reasons. I am not putting the blame on women but the new generation of most female's personality are 90% of the reasons why males cheat today. But there are men that are complete assholes that have a good woman at home but still cheat. Those type of men deserve to be in marriage jail (Not able to marry for forever) because all they will do is increase the divorce rate.

The biggest reason a man will most likely cheat is he's not satisfied at home, or his wife become fat which turns him off and another reason is he not getting along with his wife. It may be true all men think alike but we act and react differently. Some men may only cheat sexually and some others may cheat socially if that's considered cheating. If a man is not getting none or enough sex from his wife, it is in his nature to get some from somebody else. One of the biggest mistake women make is trying to punish his husband by not having sex with him for long periods of time like months just because she is upset with him. It is possible that men can wait or be patient only if he's not sexually active. But if he sexually active, he will be looking for hookers soon to satisfy his sexual needs. Trust me, he only satisfying his penis not his love. But if a man is cheating on his wife socially, like needing a conversation for satisfaction or friendship, then that means the marriage is pretty much done. Women have to think, men don't cheat by choice, only by the condition of his relationship with his wife. If a man does cheat by choice, then naturally he's a no good man and should be divorced. Sadly this generation created a belief that men are happy when they have a lot of women or they are supposed to conquer women. That's a big myth because if men was created to conquer women (to have as many women he wants), then that'll make women equal to animals which is less than a human. If the creator created one woman for Adam, He knew that a man only needs one wife. That proves that man does not need to feel like a man by having multiple women.

If a wife wants to know why her husband is cheating, she has to find where the problem is because there's an issue that needs to be resolved. If you're doing everything right and he decides to do something wrong, it's up to you to forgive him or not, but some men won't change because of the influence they had in the past when growing up. The truth is, there are men that will never cheat and there are some that will always cheat, but the non-cheater is not greater than the cheater because there's a cause and effect for everything.

Another fact is that women cheat as much as men, it's just that they are sneakier than men so they are less likely to get caught. Men are too dumb, they brag too much and always pick the wrong time, are the reason they get caught. Females become Grammy actress when they want to cheat.

They can actually cheat on their mean for like 20 years and the man will never know. Thus, the reason they say men are dogs because they know they are cats (Sneaky). Men have to get their heads out their ass for thinking that their wife or girlfriend will never cheat on them because women have the same mental impurity as men. Cheating is not only done in physical form but can happen mentally. When a man looks at another woman the way he looks at his wife; that is adultery. When a woman is having sex with her husband but fantasizes that it is someone else; that is adultery. When two couples are having physical sex with each other, they should also have it mentally and focus their mind only on each other and no one else.

But luckily America is a lot better than most countries, mainly the Middle East because women in some of those countries are forced to marry someone they don't even love. At least American women have a choice to love any man they want, but they take their choices for granted and pick their man not for love but for material wishes. The women in the middle east of the world are treated less than humans. In most Islamic countries, men are granted to marry little girls from 15 years old and young like 9 years old and there's pictures and videos that can be found on the internet of a young girl getting her head cut off because she refuse to marry a man. So basically the majority of the Middle East women are treated like sex slaves and believed to have no human purpose from their men. No women should live in fear but live in love because the one that's greater than man has loved us and didn't want us to live in fear. So it's wrong to make our women live in fear, and it's wrong to use them like a sex toy. If a man came out of women then they must be equal to them. We are naturally stronger than women because we are they protector.

This is why every woman that's born in America should have appreciation because at least they can choose whoever they want to marry. They must take care of their conscious so that they do not be brainwashed because the American television can poison a persons' mental personality because of the freedom of speech, which means everybody can have their own personality. Freedom is like everybody can read any book they want with a thousand books available. But in countries that have no freedom of speech, there's only one book to read, which the person will

never know what they are reading is right or
wrong; therefore they feel oppressed or like
a slave.

*Note: Did you know the average friend span
of female being friends are about 3 years.
The reason is because almost all females are
jealous of each other, meanwhile men are
happy for their friend's success; is the
reason men stick together 3x more than
females. Because when men cheat, they get a
high five and some bragging rights but when
women cheat, its competition. 99% of all
adult women conflict with each over men.
Anytime a female fight, it's always a man
involved or between.*

Women and their bad decisions

The majorities of women today pick
out a man base off TV, Horoscopes, books
and other misleading influences and myths;
are the reason they will never find the right
man for themselves. Most women say they

want a good man and then when they finally get one, they don't know how to deal with it and got the nerve to run around and say men aint shit. Sadly some women would completely trash good men and use the same excuse of their "Past relationships" just to say no man is good. I don't blame all females for one dumb female but females blame all men for one dumb man which is ignorant because if they took the time to find the man best for them and one that truly loves them then they wouldn't have any problems. Unfortunately some women are in heaven and still looking for hell on earth. And as soon as women can look beyond his height, his wealth, his fame, his cars; then she can find true love.

Sadly this new generation of women skips over the nice guys and goes straight for the bad guys because they seem somewhat cool. Basically most women of this generation in America are searching for one type of man instead of an individual. Shamefully a man who has a jail record will get selected before a man who has a college degree. Believe it or not that's how 80% of the world's women are. A man that is nice, respectful, understanding, compassionate, sensitive, strong minded, and faithful will be the last ones to get picked because females think they are weak. But a guy who's rude, a bully, disrespectful, unfaithful, and have bad manners will get picked first by these brainwashed women.

Most girls want that bad boy until they find themselves with kids and nowhere to go. Meanwhile the nice good man has been sitting right in front of them the whole time. But then he gets tired of waiting and so he moves on while they're stuck with kids by multiple men. See the bad decision they make early in their life will be the Karma that comes later in their life.

Unfortunately in the African American community, more women are adopting a ghetto hood rat mentality. Those types of women never appreciate a man that treats them with respect and attention, but will cheat on them with a man that calls them bitch and other insulting names. Then they got the nerve to say there are no good men in this world. If they weren't blinded by money and the material world, they would notice that it is so many good men available to them.

Note: In a relationship I always have a saying "No New Friends" the way how I see it Adults don't make "new" friends, the real true friends that we do have we have known them forever not a few months or years. So let's just be real and understand that new friends are a recipe for disaster.

The Cure

Communication

Your thoughts and feelings are hidden from each other unless you communicate them through discussions. Communication is an important part of couple sexual growth. Communication is like the heart of the relationship and what keeps the relationship going. Communication plays a huge factor in keeping a marriage healthy. Each person has 50% of the responsibility of communication.

If something is ignored, then an issue remains unresolved. The "Silent Treatment" is one of the worst punishments that you can use because it's actually a silent killer. You may think that the silent treatment is working but it's really working to cripple the relationship. Think of it like this; your marriage or whatever relationship you're in is like a computer, and you find that your computer (relationship) has viruses and the more your computer collect, the more it threatens your computer. So any small problem in your relationship is a big problem because you recognized it as a problem in the first place. Communication is an important method to use when solving problems. Don't get mixed up by confusing communication with arguments because arguments rarely solve anything but causes more problems. By raising their voice and yelling, people think that they are getting their point across when actually they forced their words across to be heard which actually builds rage or postpone the argument. The point is that a relationship without communication possibly means someone's cheating. Anybody that is too quiet in a relationship is too loud in another. Every female is talkative and talking is like their 2nd air. So if you ever notice a female being non-communicative, because she has somebody else to talk to, (which is cheating).

Forgiveness

Forgiving means letting things go and letting your mind become mature about situations. Some rather forgive and not forget but to forgive and not forget is just saving the "Situation" in your brain for later use. Saving means to bring it back up when the same situation occurs. For some people it's easy to forgive and for some others, it's hard to forgive depending on their past and life experiences. Since everybody go through different life experiences, it's impossible to judge someone who chooses to forgive or not forgive. My personal opinion is that a person should forgive and move on at the same time because if you don't forgive that person, then the pain doubles, meaning you're letting it defeat you spiritually as it already defeated you mentally. As soon as you can forgive anything then you'll realize it'll be hard to break you or your relationship. Your conscience (mind) is the most important muscle that will decide your life expectancy. No matter what the person did to you- beat you, curse you, hurt you, cheat on you, break up with you; they defeat you when you gain and use hatred from what they did to you. Forgiving problems that occurs in marriage relationships can be easy as soon you can forgive things that happened to you from your own personal life. The point is once someone cheats on you physically, you must forgive them so life can't cheat on you mentally.

Note: Unrealistic expectations are a disease to a relationship. When the expectations don't live up to its standard, a person can feel cheated, dissatisfied, and unhappy in its marriage, which later leads to someone cheated resulting to divorce. So keep in mind that a person is who they are when you first meet them.

Money Issues

If money is an issue in your relationship, Jesus said: "Who of you that wants to build a tower does not first sit down and calculate the expense, to see if he has enough to complete it. That can mean if you trying to build a relationship off of money then the relationship can collapse as soon as money problems exist. Money has always interfered with relationship and caused couples to divorce. It's true we need money to live but we don't need money to love. If money seems to be conflicting with the relationship, then both husband and wife needs to seek financial assistance and help. It's a sad thing for a married couple to break-up over money issues but it just shows that the couple wasn't meant for each other, because one may love money and the other doesn't worship it. The one who loves money will most likely put the relationship in danger because of his/her high expectations. When two people get married, they must understand that they are working together and not against each other. They must understand that "Mines and Yours" gets eliminated once married. Sure it's okay to have a few things to have on your own, especially personal things but things like food, money, house and cars should go in the "Our" category. Money is always a problem when someone doesn't know how to manage it. Money is great to have and will improve yours and your partner lifestyle, but when misused it can ruin a lot of things, including your marriage. It's simple, the one who makes more should pay more and the one who makes less should pay less to make it even. For example if the husband makes $5000 a month and the wife makes $2500 a month and the monthly rent is $1500, then it's fair that the husband pay $1000 and the wife pay $500. A caring husband makes sure his wife stays happy and knows that she likes shopping. The 50/50 rule isn't about paying the same amount but about evening out the numbers so that both sides will be happy and satisfied. Now if your partner has a gambling problem, which is dangering the relationship, he or she should seek help on that aspect. It's hard to give up the "Mines and yours" thing but when you learn that it's not competition and it's partnership, then it will be easy. Even if you make a million a year and she makes only $25,000 a year; by marrying her, you share all of that with her. God's love is way richer than our love but he shares it with us as soon we start a relationship with him. The point is money problems develop cheaters, especially women. If the relationship is focused on cash then the wife will leave as soon the husband goes broke. If a woman and man are competing with each other in a relationship, it usually means the women or the man partnered with someone else outside their relationship which is cheating. A man can buy a big house but he knows he can't build it by himself.

Note: Personal affection for each other covers a multitude of sins. If a couple really loves each other, then they will also have respect for each other. Respect is defined as "Giving Consideration to others, honoring them. A husband who takes the time to speak with his wife and really listens to what she says demonstrates his love and respect for her.

Questioning yourself

Sometimes when you stare at him while he sleeping, you ask yourself questions. Well questions only prove that you are unsure about your relationship. These are the main questions spouses ask when they are in doubt about their relationship.

1. How do I know if I am meant for the person I'm with? If you ever ask yourself or keep asking yourself "Why are you with this person", then you are not meant to be with this person, because most likely you are with

this person only to keep yourself from being lonely and bored. The result is you are going to end up cheating.

2. Why do we argue? If you argue more than you communicate, then most likely you will cheat socially. If your relationship is competition instead of partnership then it will fail resulting in someone cheating. Although Arguing is an attempt to solve an issue using anger, rage and loudness but it never cures the situation. Even though it looks like it succeeded, the uncured situation will always come back and threaten the relationship. If one bust in rage and start to raise his/her voice as soon something that ticks them off, then the relationship is in cheating mode. Since you can't ignore anything coming from the one you love, words do kill. So if your relationship has a

high rate of arguments, then therapy is needed in order to save your relationship.

Note: *Slow to speaking and slow to hearing cures arguments*

3. Why I am not turned on? If your partner doesn't turn you on or you don't get turned on, then it means you have low-sex drive and/or your partner is not sexy enough to turn you on. This results in cheating because everybody had hormones to satisfy. It also can be serious health issues that affect your sex-drive. Also, if you can't get turned on by your partner nakedness, which is the ultimate "turn on test"; then your marriage is in a divorce lane and your partner will most likely cheat by looking for "sexual satisfaction" which is hardwired in our sex organs. Maximizing your health, sexual health and looks can be the cure for "Low sex drive".

Note: *These are what you should be feeling during a relationship- Pleased, Happy, Glad, Aroused, Confident, Fascinated, Overwhelmed, Intense, Excited, Surprised, Joyful, Playful, Calm, Thoughtful; and if your relationship has achieved all of these feelings, then your relationship is successful or slightly perfect. If you have none of these feelings, it means someone's cheating.*

Note: Exercise Together: Exercising together puts your marriage in better shape than anything. You and your partner burning fat together, gaining muscles together, sweating together and getting tired together can lead both of you taking a shower together, and that's how every exercise should end. So get up and jog around the park together, do some aerobics and get that heart pumping. Exercising also improves both of your sexual health.

Solving Minor Problems

Minor Problems: Small problems grow bigger when they go unresolved. Every problem needs to be treated as soon it's mentioned. A partner may not want to be petty by bringing a small issue up but deep inside it has an effect on him/her. So it's a good idea to communicate on everything. Minor issues such as the wife burns food, the husband has smelly feet, the wife leaves her pads in the bathroom or the husband use too much soap when washing dishes; can all be fix using calm communication. Now if one doesn't want to change, then that person doesn't want his relationship to improve and then the problems will get bigger. Small issues and big issues may not be the same weight but both direct you into failure. It takes practice and determination to remain calm when discussing hurt feelings, misunderstandings, and personal feelings.

Solving problems helps develop stronger intimacy and brings the couple closer. So in conclusion, make sure you and your partner put time, patient and dedication in solving any type of minor problems to improve the quality of your relationship.

Note: Pray: Praying helps and heals the negative things going on in your life. So get down on your knees and pray with your partner and God will answer both of you at the same time, hopefully. But don't just pray when you're sad and mad, pray when you're happy and glad.

Looks

Looks can be the biggest reason a person cheats. A couple needs to understand that their partner looks will change from time. If you pick your partner solely from the way he/she looks then you'll most likely be disappointed when your partner profile changes. Ladies, remember when that guy came up to you and ask you for your name and then your number. Then after a couple of weeks, you and him are in a relationship. Well think about this, that guy didn't approach you and ask you for your name and number because he liked your personality; he hardly knew you. He didn't approach you because the way you smell because he couldn't smell you from afar. He didn't approach you because you can cook; he never tasted your cooking before. That guy who is your husband today only approached you because he liked what he saw; in other words, you were beautiful to him. So it's clear that men select females base off their looks first. So for a woman to change her looks (like get out of shape) during her relationship with the man who chose her for her looks first, is an insult to the man and that can put the relationship in danger. Thus be the main reason a man will cheat. So the solution to that problem is to only let "age" change the way you look. Cutting your hair, gaining weight purposely, getting piercings or tattoos, getting plastic surgeries or anything that make you unattractive to him can danger the relationship and result to her man looking at other women.

Note: A relationship that is not intimate is not real

Sex

Bad sex can be the number one reason a person cheats on their significant other. If problems exist in the bedroom with sex, it can destroy the relationship but there's always a way to improve your sexual relationship with your partner. A healthy sexual relationship is like the icing on the cake in the relationship. If one is sexually active and the other is not, then the relationship will never work because the one that is sexually active will cheat. Both male and female have to be sexually active in order to have a healthy relationship. Sexuality is about sharing pleasure, not passing a performance test, so men learn to please your women naturally without taking harmful drugs. There is more to sex and sexuality than your penis, intercourse, and orgasm. Sexuality is about sharing and enjoying affection, pleasuring, intimate playfulness, eroticism, intercourse, orgasm, tenderness and passion for life. As soon as both sides understand that, then their sex life will improve and will see that it's more than in and out (intercourse), and busting a nut. Sex with love and affection has a way better orgasm than just sex, a quickie or "get it over with sex". The key to successful sex is to relax, slow down and enjoy the pleasuring process and not rush intercourse or orgasms.

Note: *Sexuality is an integral, positive part of you and it includes your attitudes, emotions, behavior, body image, physical well-being, values and how you feel about your relationship. Sometimes sex is a tension/stress reducer, sometimes it's a way to share closeness; sometimes it's a quick passionate encounter, sometimes it's a way to heal an argument, sometimes it reduce emotional distance. In reality, sex is often better for one partner than the other.*

Note: *A husband and a wife must understand that their partner's emotional and sexual feelings are very important. It is essential to heal the emotional pain because your relationship feelings are the energy source for your sexual relationship. When both put the other's feelings and happiness first, the emotional benefits can be wonderful.*

Understanding Sex

Understanding sex is as important as living life. Sex is healthy, a good stress reliever and natural. The most important sex organ in your body is your mind because sex is done more mentally than physically. Both have to be into it in order to be at peak, but if one of the partner not interested, then the overall performance will flop. Neither one should force their partner to do anything that they are not interested in because that will most likely scar the relationship. So before you fall in love and get in a relationship with someone, make sure you two agree on everything about sex because if you marry a person who doesn't give head and you like receiving head then you'll have problems during your relationship and it may result to adultery. That's why sex is a major part of a relationship. Don't watch porn, if you don't know by now porn can ruin a relationship for a couple who's been married even 30 years. It has a negative influence and creates urges to cheat on your partner and besides the sex in porn is not real, it's edited. So if you want to strengthen your relationship with your partner, avoid Porn at all cost because the moment you watch other people have sex you'll start to commit fornication consciously, making your mind wonder in wicked ways. If you just trying to get a hard on, it only means your partner is not attractive anymore even when naked. If my wife says she has to watch some porn to get in the mood, I'll consider that as an insult because dropping my Hanes should be enough for her. So if you are a man and can't get a "hard on" or if you a woman and can't get wet, only physical changes need to be made.

Note: *It is normal to have sexual difficulties on occasion, so women it's better to be patient with him instead of throwing him under the fire and ruin the relationship.*

Preparing for Sex

Would you eat a meal an hour before you play basketball or a track meet? No, right, so since sex is like aerobic exercise, it's a good idea not to eat anything before sex and most definitely not to load up on sugar as it deploys the urge to be active. Best bet is drinking ginseng or vitamin water an hour before you get into it. It's also good to stretch out your legs and arms for better performance and blood flow. Try not to stress over anything and just think about the nakedness of your partner and what you would like to do to him or her. If you need extra help to feel the urge, try phone sex with your partner first and then when she/he walks in the door you should be more than ready. If you need to spice things up, send naughty texts back and forth all day until you two get home and finish the story. Play strip trivia- ask each other questions and whoever answers wrong has to strip off a piece of clothing. Have a lap dance. Send naked photos to each other, creating a higher desire. But this can be dangerous, I advise couples to delete pictures after it's been seen already. Record the sounds of your moans when having sex with each other, then when you two get home, play the sound on your cd player. Make your kisses more passionate. Have sex blindfold. Use food like ice pops and whip cream and blueberries. Play wrestle with no clothes on, and whoever gets pinned or tap out has to let their lover take control. Bite and nibble for 10 minutes. Slip a donut on his penis and slowly lick it off. Be careful with fantasy dress-up sex because some imaginations can create a negative desire.

NOTE: To keep your relationship healthy, have sex daily or at least 3 times a week. If you wait too long to have sex again you can lose desire in your mate and see him/her as unattractive. Females, if you want to keep your man, overdose him and make sure he's addicted to you, and be careful with that vaginal probation crap. That doesn't works, only gives a man a reason to cheat.

Places to have Sex

Sometimes you want to extend your sex life somewhere else other than the bedroom. The shower is the most relaxing place to have sex. It's like getting a massage and getting an orgasm at the same time. Especially if you have back problems, while the warm water crashing against your back, you're enjoying your penetration with your partner. If you got the freak in you and want to enjoy a freaky moment, then car sex or in the back seat of your car is perfect to get all the freakiness out of you to release some stress. Don't worry; being a freak means you're healthy and sexually active. Those who are not a freak in the bed are most likely the worst lovers, and when they have an orgasm it's nothing. So be a freak and have some freak sex. I don't prefer floor sex unless you have very strong knees and back, and a soft carpet. Since floor sex is the cause of many back aches and pains I avoid this unless I have a sleeping bag. A sleeping bag is perfect for the cold days and it keeps you and your partner close together. Park sex; hey don't be a shame because in the historic days when there were no houses, that's when making babies took place. Parks and gardens were called homes to people B.C. So go head and give a park a chance to take your sex to exceed your limits. It's fun, beautiful and the air makes it better. But you should not do it in front of people because sex is personal and should only be seen by the only two people that are doing it. Other good places to have sex are the Jacuzzi, inside a paddle boat, on the roof top, in a cave and on a beach should help maximize your sex life.

NOTE: The only way to make sure your sexual relationship is at the strongest peak, if you or your partner is not embarrass of each other nakedness and that you two are having great sex. If you and your partner is married and she or he still comes out the shower with a towel covering his/her body when it's just you two in the house, then that should tell you that your relationship is weak. A good relationship is confident, trusted, honest, loving and happy. If you don't feel any one of these, then you might have to make a decision. Also when having sex, don't fall into a pattern of routine (mechanical sex) which make sex becomes low priority and less interesting. Then later falls into the cycle of low-sex or no sex marriage.

Can women and men be friends?

The question I always asked is, for what reason any guy wants to hang out with a woman? No man should have anything in common with females unless he's homosexual. Men hang with men and women hang with women and that's the way nature had it to be. I'm pretty sure if you are a man; you don't want your wife hanging out with other men even though they "went to high school together". The only exception is if they are related. So if a man is gay then yes he has a common personality that allows him to hang around females, and if a girl is a dike, then she also has a common personality to hang out with a man. But if they are both straight, it's going to end when one gets in a relationship.

I think the real question should be; can females and men friendship last? Maybe in high school or middle school and as teenagers but when girls and boys become adults, everything changes. No man should hang around another man's wife and no women should hang around married men because that ruins relationships and families. So yes boys and girls can be friends up until they get married. Think about this, if you out of high school and out of college, think about all the female friends you had that are now married or in a serious relationship, what you think they would say if you ask them to go to a party with you or to the movies? It makes perfect sense because there is no reason to be spending majority of your time nurturing a friendship with a friend of the opposite sex. Your significant other should fill that role. Unless you are keeping them as a back-up if your relationship fails. Men and women can be friends temporary but the best friend thing doesn't work. What most females don't understand is that the attraction and "best friend" belong only to their boyfriend or husband. If you don't see your boyfriend or husband as your best friend then you're not in a real relationship.

Maybe I got the wrong idea of a female friend but from my experience I see that being friends with females especially when they single, they'll show you 100% love. But then when they get a boyfriend or get back with their ex, they automatically close the door on you like feelings don't exist. This is why I feel if I befriend a girl we shouldn't get too close. All I'm trying to say is I want something out of the time I put into because you can't get that time back. It's basically like insurance for love. It takes a lot of feelings for a man to love someone, that's why it's hard for us to just turn it off like that.

Honestly I believe that men and women can be friends for a short period of time because once that woman gets a boyfriend; she will no longer be a friend to him. Remember, being a friend consist of spending quality time, not being an associate that speaks once a month. Think about it, the meaning of friends for guys is not the same meaning of friends for a girl. A friend for a women means the guy is useful in many ways like for entertainment purposes, movie partners and financial reasons. A friend for a guy means to stick with him through it all even when they get married to different people. Also sometimes a man will expect his lady friend to accept the "Friends with benefits" clause or they can't be truly friends. One of the main reasons a guy and girl can't be friends because the man main focus is sex in any relationship. His lady friend might not think it, but he's thinking of having sex with her all the time and will take any chances he gets once she flirts. When they first met, his first thought was, "she look good, how can I hit it" and he thought of having sex with her more than once, he just didn't tell her. Sadly this is the way American men are brought up thinking that they have to conquer women by having sex with them. Women today are brought up to take as much as she can from men before giving it up to them, basically prostituting themselves legally. Television and other negative influences spoiled our minds with mass sexual activities that lead to divorce later on in our lives.

Some believe if there's no physical attraction, then true friendship is possible. It's somewhat true because if I'm attractive to a lady friend, I most likely would want something more between us, but if I don't find her physically attractive, then it's possible to be just friends for a short period of time. I think this applies to most guys; I mean why in the world would you just want to be friends with a gorgeous girl? But even when you think you not attracted to a friend, you will be because overtime attraction grows and you start looking at people differently. When you spend extended periods of time with someone of the opposite sex (and you both are straight), both of you are very likely to start developing feelings. Logically, feelings create attraction, attraction creates desires and urges, and if you dare to fight an urge everyday of your life, you will fail.

Excuse me for a sec; I just want to throw this in here. For the guys that accept the friend zone are suckers because what guy puts women in friend zones? Females created that just to put guys to the side in case the one they're focusing in front of them fails. Basically friend zones means back up or it can mean "save for later". That's why females are so wishful in believing a guy and a girl can be friends just to get what they want. Men has to understand that female get asked to have sex just about every day of their life so they're naturally overwhelmed by guys that they're used to it. So females secretly spend a lot of time choosing the guys that they want to be with sexually, and the guys they put in the friend zone is like a waiting line in heaven to see if they going to get the "yes or no". But men don't get asked to have sex everyday by a female unless they are a celebrity, so they naturally go out doing all the asking. So females has to understand that men are not thirsty for sex, we don't choose females to have sex with but you females do all the choosing and can get sex whenever you want.

The bottom line is men and women can be friends for a short period of time like only in middle school or high school. If you still doubting, then ask yourself this question first and you will get the answer. Can the rich and poor be friends? That should give you the sufficient answer to that question. The only successful way of both genders being friends is if they both totally unattracted to each other and one is gay and the other is a lesbian. If you think about it, it must be true that men and women can't be friends because we ask this question all the time.

The point of this chapter is to strengthen the marriage relationships so that the brainwashers or porn doesn't ruin it as the New World Order has a conspiracy to destroy all natural marriages.

Chapter 10

Make-Up in Disguise

Another part of the New World Order conspiracy involves massive use of Cosmetics. Cosmetics used on children was first to promote child porn and induce adults into buying children in sex rings. The thousands of children that go missing every year are forced to wear make-up to appear more attracted to adults so the pimps could get their money. Read more

There is an Identity crisis going on in America from our women, and Cosmetics is the ring leader for the most cause. Women today spend billions of dollars to fix their low self-esteem by applying expensive chemical filled make-up, which is hiding in an artificial mask just to be seen by the public. Today Cosmetics are being applied to mislead and deceive to become worshipped by men. And while we are commercializing Make-ups and promoting it on TV, video games and children books; we are sexualizing our kids since make-up is use to attract men. The fake breast, the fake hair, the fake nails, the fake personality, Botox, plastic surgery shows that women has lost all of their sense of identity. They rarely know who they are because when they finally look in the mirror after they take the make-up off, they barely recognize themselves. One of the poor excuses most women make just to put on make-up is that they always say their face is boring, but in reality it's only boring if you don't know what you're looking at.

The cosmetics industry makes billions of dollars annually. Fashion and Hollywood have set the standards for "beauty," making it seem important to be fashionable. But is painting your face "fashionable" to God? Of course, some have no interest in what God says because the Bible has no meaning or value to them. They are not concerned with pleasing God but are only interested in pleasing themselves and other people. The sad part is that wearing make-up has become a worldwide custom that been accepted all over. Therefore, to even question the use of makeup may seem old-fashioned or outdated to countless millions of women and men too-who have grown accustomed to and comfortable with its widespread use. Unfortunately make-up is used everywhere that every time you turned on the television, watched a movie or go outside, there is a form of cosmetic.

The last couple of decades have become a make-up progress from its early days to become an art and an important part of beauty-setting false standards of beauty. Then at the turn of the twentieth century, make-up was viewed as something only proud women wore. With the invention of movies and television, Hollywood injected into the limelight the image of a movie starlet's face covered with cosmetics. Once this image was accepted by the masses, cosmetics became common priority. Then the movie industry became the most responsible for associating make-up with exquisite beauty, by turning actresses into a fantasy. It influences young girls and adult women to look like world-famous screen idols. Now millions of female fans want to look like their favorite movie stars, not knowing they became slaves to fashion trends. Even little girls can become obsessed with being pretty, when they should be enjoying childhood and getting education.

Cover girl magazines trick people into buying an illusion- something that simply does not exist. What nobody thinks about is that they always use models in their 20's when older people spend more money trying to look like them. These magazines brainwash women into thinking they aren't completely dressed until they complete their face with make-up. Also, Cover girl magazines are meant to sell products by giving women false thoughts of themselves of not being pretty enough naturally and have to buy their products. Adding to the fact that it influences women to have poor self-esteem about their image and believing make-up is the cure. Even though anyone can be made into a cover girl, no one looks like a "cover model" even the cover models. The models and celebrities you see in magazines don't look like that in real life either. They have flaws just like the rest of us. Being dolled up to go out on the town, they don't look anywhere near what they do in their photo spreads.

A 15 year old girl doesn't stop to think that the photos she compares herself to are fake, photo shopped. She accepts them at face value and wonders why she can't look like that. This is the reason why most girls are brainwashed because they keep looking at fake models and fake celebrities and think they are perfect. Then we wonder why our teenagers are having problems adjusting to society because we (adults) don't tell them how beautiful they are and tell them that any good make-up artist can take a woman off the street and turn her into a cover girl.

African females are suffering the most. Sadly Malcolm X didn't live long enough to influence the African American females to be themselves. They are brainwashed to hate the way they look so they destroy their natural hair by putting perms into it just to make it straight, which kills the hair cells in a couple of years. The way black men use to make their hair straight, black women are now doing the same thing to make them appear more "White". God made people the way they are, not meant to have surgeries or to change your physical features. If you was born with thick hair, he designed it just for you, if you was born with soft hair, it was meant for you. Also African American women are taking it too far by bleaching their skin and using skin lightening creams just to make them appear to be a model. Mostly African American Women celebrities use these false tactics to sell more products, sadly because America favors the lighter skin. Most African American women put perms in their hair, which results in balding and hair loss, most White Women get sun tans, which results in skin cancer, Spanish women wear excessive make-up, which results in early wrinkles and aging fast. The point is all women of color have lost sense of identity, especially African American women. Why does a black woman wants to look white? Why does some white wants to be dark? And why does Puerto Ricans wants to look older? It shows you that the low self-esteem is high in the beauty compartment. Women are chasing perfection but if God already made you in his image, then you are not chasing perfection but more imperfection.

What are the ingredients in Make-up?

Some of the ingredients in cosmetics are hazardous to your health. Many of these ingredients are also used in industrial manufacturing processes to clean industrial equipment, stabilize pesticides and grease gears. Sadly, the FDA allows the cosmetics industry to put thousands of synthetic chemicals into personal care products, even if those chemicals are linked to cancer, infertility or birth defects. At the same time as untested chemicals have been steadily introduced into our environment, breast cancer incidence has risen dramatically. The truth is many of the ingredients in make-up are dangerous. Researchers have found that over 10,000 ingredients used in cosmetic are hazardous industrial chemicals. This means that 10,000 industrial chemicals are used as cosmetic ingredients, many of which are carcinogens, pesticides, reproductive toxins, endocrine disruptors, plasticizers (chemicals that keep concrete soft), degreasers (used to get grime off auto parts) and surfactants (they reduce surface tension in water, like in paint and inks). And these go on our skin and into the environment

Butyl acetate

Butyl acetate is found in nail strengtheners and nail polishes.

Health Hazards: Butyl acetate vapors may cause dizziness or drowsiness. Continued use of a product containing butyl acetate may cause skin to crack and become dry.

Butylated hydroxytoluene

Butylated hydroxytoluene is found in a

variety of cosmetics and personal care products. It is an antioxidant which helps slow the rate at which a product changes color over time.

Health Hazards: Butylated hydroxytoluene may cause skin and eye irritation.

Coal tar

Coal tar is used to control itching and scaling, to soften skin, and as a colorant.

Health Hazards: Coal tar is a human carcinogen.

Other hazardous ingredients are

Parabens, Used in makeup, moisturizers, shampoos etc. May interfere with hormone function. Associated with breast cancer. Look out for ingredients with "paraben" in their name (methylparaben, butylparaben, propylparaben, isobutylparaben, ethylparaben). Widely used even though they are known to be toxic.

DEA, Cocamide, Lauramide, in creamy and foaming products such as moisturizer, shampoo. Can react to form cancer-causing nitrosamines. Harmful to fish and other wildlife.

Dibutyl Phthalate or DBP, in nail products and some hair sprays. Toxic to reproduction and may interfere with hormone function. Harmful to fish and other wildlife.

BHA (butylated hydroxyanisole) and BHT (butylated hydroxytoluene in moisturizer, makeup, etc. Can cause cancer and interfere with hormone function. Harmful to fish and other wildlife.

, Coal Tar Dyes: Look for P-PHENYLENEDIAMINE in hair dyes and colors identified as "C.I." followed by five digits in other products. Potential to cause cancer and can be contaminated with heavy metals toxic to the brain.

, Formaldehyde-Releasing Preservatives...Look for DMDM HYDANTOIN, DIAZOLIDINYL UREA, IMIDAZOLIDINYL UREA, METHENAMINE, or QUARTERNIUM-15. Widely used in hair products, moisturizers, etc. Formaldehyde causes cancer...,

Synthetic fragrances and Parfum: Widely

used even in some products marketed as "unscented" (often the last ingredient). Mixture of chemicals that can trigger allergies and asthma. Some linked to cancer and neurotoxicity. Some harmful to fish and other wildlife

PEGs (polyethylene glycols): Widely used in conditioners, moisturizers, deodorants, etc. Can be contaminated with 1, 4-dioxane, which can cause cancer

Petrolatum: In hair products, lip balm/lipstick, skin care products. Petroleum product that can be contaminated with cancer-causing impurities

Mineral Oil :(Most harmful when poorly refined) in many other care products such as baby oil, body lotions, soap and makeup. Mineral oil is a petroleum by-product which clogs the pores and interferes with the skin's ability to eliminate toxins, promoting acne and other disorders. Slows down skin function and cell development, resulting in premature aging. May be contaminated with PAHs (carcinogens).

Siloxanes: (Cyclomethicone and ingredients ending in "siloxane" (e.g., cyclotetrasiloxane) widely used in moisturizer, makeup, hair products, etc. Can interfere with hormone function and damage the liver. Harmful to fish and other wildlife.

Sodium Lauryl Sulfate (SLS) and Sodium Laureth Sulfate (SLES): In products that foam such as shampoo, cleansers, bubble bath. SLES can be contaminated with 1, 4-dioxane, which may cause cancer. SLS may damage liver. Irritates skin, eyes and respiratory tract. Harmful to fish and other wildlife.

Triclosan: In "anti-bacterial" products such as toothpaste, soaps, hand sanitizers. May interfere with hormone function. Harmful to fish and other wildlife.

Chemical Sunscreens (with Retinyl Palmitate, Oxybenzone and Octyl Methoxycinnamate): When many of the chemicals used in popular sunscreens are exposed to sunlight, reactions occur between the sunscreen's active and inactive ingredients and the epidermis. Toxic reactions include inflammation, dermalogical effects, allergic reactions and photogenotoxic (DNA altering) effects.

Chemical sunscreens have ingredients that actually promote cancer.

Aluminum: Aluminum is a common ingredient in deodorant and mostly antiperspirant. It is often linked to Alzheimer's and brain disorders and is a possible risk factor in breast cancer. Aluminum-based compounds in antiperspirants form a temporary plug within the sweat duct that stops the flow of sweat to the skin's surface, which forces toxins to flow back into the bloodstream.

Heavy Metals: Lead, Mercury, Cadmium, Arsenic, Nickel and More: Heavy metals can build up in the body over time and are known to cause varied health problems, which can include: cancer, reproductive and developmental disorders, neurological problems; memory loss; mood swings; nerve, joint and muscle disorders; cardiovascular, skeletal, blood, immune system, kidney and renal problems; headaches; vomiting, nausea, and diarrhea; lung damage; contact dermatitis; and brittle hair and hair loss. Many are suspected hormone disruptors and respiratory toxins, and for some like lead, there is no known safe blood level.

Talc: Commonly found in baby powders, face powders, body powders. Talc is a known carcinogen and is a major cause of ovarian cancer. It can be harmful if inhaled as it can lodge in the lungs, causing respiratory disorders. Since the early 1980s, records show that several thousand infants each year have died or become seriously ill following accidental inhalation of baby powder.

What does the bible says about wearing make-up

Jeremiah 4:30 you should not enlarge your eyes with paint? In vain you beautify yourself. Your lovers despise you; they seek your life. Those lusting after you have rejected you; they keep seeking for your very soul.

One of the reasons it is a sin to wear makeup, because Jezebel and other prostitutes covered their face in make-up to seduce men and to lie with them, and God considered them as whores of the nation. All the good women in the bible didn't wear any. But let's read more what the bible says.

Note: In biblical days a man could divorce his wife if he learned that his wife had worn makeup during their courtship, thereby misleading him about her appearance.

Vanity—the desire to look more beautiful—is what causes women to paint their faces, and is perhaps the most powerful of human drives.

Vanity

Read **Psalms 39:5-6**

Pride and vanity is your negative conscience. Today, the desire to look better, smell better and feel better causes consumers worldwide—mostly women—to spend an estimated $65 billion annually on false advertised cosmetics". Most women want to look beautiful by the wrong standards. Even young girls are unhappy with themselves to the point of depression. They feel that they do not measure up to their peers or favorite movie stars. Sadly younger and younger girls who enter beauty contests are also having cosmetic surgery just to attempt to win the contest. What they don't know is the ignorance of injecting tiny amounts of deadly poison, Botox (from botulism); under the skin of the face to remove wrinkles have consequences. Within four days, the toxin in the treatment literally paralyzes the facial muscles and temporarily smoothes the skin. (The treatments only last for 90 days.) The goal is to "look the best you can for as long as you can". It is as though we given up on authenticy. Instead of a financial theft it's more like a self-identity theft.

THE HISTORY OF MAKE-UP

The use of cosmetics is very ancient dating to biblical times. By the 1st century AD the Egyptian, Roman, Greek and Middle Eastern cultures had developed cosmetics such as powders to whiten the skin; kohl to darken the eyelids, eyelashes, and eyebrows; rouge for the cheek. Egyptian tombs represent the earliest recorded references to the use of make-up but were by no means the only culture to use it. Here are some specifics: During the Predynastic period [ending in 3200 B.C.], men as well as women applied a line of green paint around the eyes…In dynastic times the color of paint used was a dark gray. Red ochre seems to have been used to color the cheeks and henna the palms, nails, and, in the late period at least, the hair. Assyrians resorted to black dye for eyebrows, hair and beard, whereas the Persians used henna, which produced an orange-red color, a style that existed from 1900 BC. Gold dust, gold thread, and scented yellow starch were sometimes used in the hair and beard for festive occasions

Even before its use in Egypt, the original painted harlot was Semiramis, the mother-wife of Nimrod, and the founder of the Babylonian Mystery Religion. Semiramis is known as the mother of all harlots. She used make-up and whorish clothing for various religious and sexual rituals. The following quote describes the kind of seductive, sensual clothing that she and later the Egyptians wore: "Modern knowledge of ancient Egyptian dress derives for the most part from ancient paintings and sculpture, since very few garments have been preserved…The earliest representations of women show them either nude or clad in tightly fitting white linen skirts down to the ankles. Also Nudity linked the use of make-up. Along with various statues, paintings and busts still in existence from ancient times, descriptions show how Egyptians used cosmetics and revealing clothing to appeal to their sensuality. They adopted this dress into their culture from Semiramis, in an attempt to appear more like the many gods and goddesses they worshipped.

The use of cosmetics spread from culture to culture. Each civilization adopted its own methods of applying and producing cosmetics. The following shows how the Assyrian, Babylonian, Persian and Greek cultures all took their lead from Egypt. Notice: "preparations were externally applied to change or enhance the beauty of skin, hair, nails, lips, and eyes. The use of body paint for ornamental and religious purposes has been common…The Egyptians used kohl to darken their eyes; a crude paint was used on the face, and fingers were often dyed with henna…Beauty aids reached a peak in imperial Rome—especially chalk for the face. Pride and Vanity was evolving all over.

Many women who used cosmetics in these cultures were for the purpose of prostitution. History shows how women applied make-up to change their appearance and seduce men. Harlots and "matrons" (the female leaders of prostitution rings) were specifically recognized by their silk, jewels and cosmetics. Women who used cosmetics in ancient Sparta were specifically known for being prostitutes: "Women wore brightly colored dresses, a lot of cosmetic, which a woman could do only if she earned her living through prostitution. It is clear that the first women to wear makeup were prostitutes! Changing one's appearance by facial paint to hide their identity and to deceive men. Cosmetics were nothing more than a device used by harlots to, in effect, teaches men to break the Seventh Commandment.

Jeremiah 4:30

Now that the history of cosmetics has been discovered, let's ask this question. What does the Bible say about it?

Some people say they never seen a reference to make-up in the Bible because the actual words "make-up", "cosmetics", "lipstick", are not found in the Bible, but direct references to make-up and eye paint are found . After reviewing them, you will be convinced that make-up is a disguise. Jeremiah 4:30 means God is condemning His people for abominations within their conduct and their behavior. One of the abominations that God hates is painting the face—thereby taking on the nature of a prostitute. The whole point in verse 30 is that painting the eyes is a common method of a prostitute. Sadly, women of today may think they just want to "look nice" to the world, when they really look like prostitutes to God.

Read **Ezekiel 23:2 to verse 40**. This is an incredible series of verses. God directly likens Israel and Judah (seeking allies among the nations) to harlots who have sent for men after painting their faces—exactly like whores awaiting their next customers. This is a clear, unmistakable condemnation of the use of eye make-up. Next, God issues a sentence to all who have committed spiritual crimes (sins) in His sight. "'This therefore is the Lord the eternal's sentence: Bring a host of folk against them, and hand them over to be maltreated and robbed! Let them be stoned and put to the sword…that all women may take warning and avoid your sensual way and learn that I am the Lord the eternal!'" Women of the modern world, you can see that God connects eye paint directly to seduction for harlotrous purposes.

Isaiah 3:16-17

Because the daughters of Zion are haughty, and walk with stretched forth necks and wanton eyes…Therefore the Lord will smite with a scab the crown of the head of the daughters of Zion, and the Lord will discover their secret parts"…

"Wanton eyes" as "…to blink in a flirty way." This obviously means using the eyes for seductive purposes.

The meaning of "wanton": "Immoral or unchaste; lewd." But what makes the eyes "immoral or lewd"?

Wanton eyes—Hebrew (mesha-ququeroth, from shaquar, to deceive), 'deceiving with their eyes.'...Lowth, after the Chaldaic, 'falsely setting off the eyes with paint.' Women's eyelids in the East are often colored with stibium, or powder of lead."

While no one realizes this, vanity is a form of natural desire for worship and adoration from other people. Though it springs from inferiority, vanity is the human method of covering this feeling by elevating oneself above others. Only GOD is to be worshipped and adored! When people take this to themselves, it is a form of idolatry and directly violates the Second Commandment.

The study of makeup would be incomplete without examining one of the most evil women in the Old Testament—Jezebel—and her use of cosmetics. This infamous woman was both a queen and a prophetess who practiced witchcraft. Jezebel endeavored to improve the appearance of her complexion by paint…This casts light enough on Jezebel's painting…and shows sufficiently with what design she did it, to conquer and disarm Jehu, and induce him to take her for wife…This staining of the eye with stibium and painting was a universal custom, not only in Asiatic countries, but also in all those that bordered on them, or had connections with them". When Jehu came to Jezreel and Jezebel heard of it, 'she put her eyes into lead polish (painted them with it), and beautified her head and placed herself at the window'…It is prepared from antimony ore…which when pounded yields a black powder with a metallic brilliancy, which was laid upon the eyebrows and eyelashes. The object was to heighten the splendor of the dark southern eye, and give it a more deeply glowing fire, and to impart a youthful appearance to the whole of the eyelashes even in extreme old age. "Jehu then immediately went to Jezreel to execute Jezebel. Her make-up failed to seduce him and her abominations came to an end when Jehu had her thrown from a window. The dogs did eat her flesh as God had declared.

Think carefully. Consider those who wore makeup: the false prophetess Jezebel, two whoring sisters, Aholah and Aholibah, and the adulteress Judah are the only Bible examples of women (real or by analogy) who wore make-up. Now think of the most well-known, righteous women of the Bible. Name a single one (Old or New Testament) who wore make-up. There is no mention of Sarah, Rebecca, Ruth, Naomi, Mary (Christ's mother), Deborah, Abigail, Esther or any other virtuous woman ever applying or wearing make-up. The fact that the only examples of those who wore make-up are adulteresses, harlots and false prophetesses serves as a great warning to anyone who cares about the Word of God and wishes to follow the Bible's righteous examples instead of the wicked.

Does God want you to "look more beautiful" than you are? Does He want you to attempt to improve on what He made? Let's read what God says!

God created our original parents, Adam and Eve, in the Garden of Eden. Genesis 1:27 states, "So God created man in His own image, in the image of God created Him…male and female." God made human beings to look like Himself, to be in His image. And there is certainly no biblical record of God or Christ ever wearing cosmetics. He did not feel that Eve's eyelids needed to be light green or that her lips needed to be painted bright red, purple or any other unnatural color. Trying to improve your face through facial paint is telling God, "I am not happy with the way you made me," or, after applying make-up, asking Him, "Why didn't you make me like this. If God had meant for women to appear as they do after painting their faces, He would have designed their faces this way from creation. Make-up appeals to both the sense of sight and vanity. Women wear cosmetics because they feel this makes them look more attractive. By this feeling of increased beauty, their vanity swells. This is exactly what happened to Satan.

Finally, David said, "Turn away mine eyes from beholding vanity" (119:37), and "Remove far from me vanity and lies" (Prov.30:8). Wearing make-up is a form of deceit and deceit is a lie. God is concerned with our character, not customizations of our appearance. He is far more interested in the beauty of your heart than your clothes. If your character is pure and attractive, then you are properly attired in God's sight.

However, it is not wrong to wear jewelry, in Ezekiel 16, attired ancient Israel in beautiful clothes and jewels. Jewelry is not sin, as with alcohol, cards, dancing and other activities. It is not the activity that is wrong, but rather the wrong use of the activity.

Make-up is done to get more beauty, attention and more looks from others for selfish reasons. Wearing make-up is an addiction. Billions of dollars are spent because the world is addicted to vanity. Wearing make-up in moderation is to say that one can sin in moderation. There is absolutely nowhere in the Bible where God allows for even a little bit of sin. Ladies, God is concerned with what kind of a person you are inside. This is what makes a woman truly beautiful. He is not concerned with outward beauty, and labels painted women as whores. To naturally look beautiful, you have to be healthy. You have to eat fresh fruits and vegetables to help nourish the skin. Junk food adds to the natural imperfections you already have. The price of junk food helps you age quicker and sags your skin. People are beautiful when the inner beauty of the person shines through. What makes a girl ugly is when she thinks she too pretty. Lastly, we have to teach our young girls that beauty is only skin deep and how you take care of yourself. You eat junk food you become and look like junk food. You eat fruits and vegetables you will look fresh all the time without the make-up. And inner happiness is what counts, because happy girls are the prettiest.

Chapter 11
Read between the lines

The First chapter of this book (Evolution) shows you how to respect this chapter. The 2nd chapter trains you how to think and open up a new path for your thoughts. The 3rd chapter relates to this chapter but gives you a new eye to see. The 4th chapter helps you understand the meaning of NWO. The 5th and 6th chapter shows you their favorite victims. The 7th chapter explains the affects and what is happening now. The 8th chapter explains a part of their plan. The 9th chapter guides you in defeating one major part of the system. And the 10th chapter discovers another major conspiracy in their plan.

Finding yourself creates a beautiful mind and a beautiful mind makes a beautiful life. There's nothing clearer than seeing the world through your own eyes and being able to have enhanced judgment of your own ears, because people are like music, some speak the truth and others just make noise. To listen with your own ears also includes secret access to enjoyable sounds because the earth also has music for those who listens. Sadly people follow a trend and nod their head when they are told to. Those people are not listening with their own ears and seeing with their own eyes. This time an eye for an eye don't have to make the whole world blind. Take note: the signs on a dollar pretends to be far from our eyes. We think we're trading it for goods but more likely for our souls. The only reason money makes the world go round because the devil is on a shopping spree and it shames me that people are hopping in his cart for free. But I'm not going to judge someone who sins differently from me when we all are sad when we pray but happy when we sin. So my main goal is to take the chains off our minds so our thoughts can wander freely instead of going in a circle of a maze. I know I will fall short every time but it's nothing like striving for perfection that's why my main objective in life is to be successful through God. The keys to being successful starts in the morning when you wake up. When the alarm clock goes off you have a choice, to either get up or hit the snooze button. That will determine if you really want to be successful. Getting up means you want to work for success, snoozing means you rather go back to sleep and dream of being successful. Another key to success is to ignore the jealousy, the backlash, the hate. People are going to talk bad about you until the day you die. As long as they see you doing well, they are going to throw stones until you fall, so it's up to you to build a solid empire with the bricks they have thrown at you. The last key to success is instead of wiping away your tears; wipe away the people that are causing them. Destroy what destroys you, and if nobody gives you a boost then build your own latter. Those are some of the keys to success. Success is those who are their own boss and those who think for themselves. Don't forget that every successful person lived by the clock. Everything was done by time; on time; overtime and too much time. I'm not saying it's easy, all you have to do is put your mind into it. No one ever died from thinking but many lost their lives due to lack of thought. Therefore you have to find a way to turn your mind into a clock with unlimited time; then you will find success.

Sadly, many of you have opportunities but depend on dreams. Life is about taking chances to get success. If you're not taking chances then you're still wandering in the maze.

You never run out of chances, only confidence. That's when you allow the brainwashers to put a limit to your chances. If the chances you want to take aren't deadly or negative, then you have nothing to lose but opportunity. Sometimes it's hard and painful to be successful but that's when prayer helps. When I'm struggling, I pray. Even If I still fail, I am over blessed. The blessings that I have are countless; that's why I don't understand why people try to count their blessings. The blessings are like the number of stars in space. If a person tries to count all their blessings, that person would run out of breath. For the past 30 years I woke up in the morning. 30x365 is

10,950 blessings that happened in the morning. And that's only 1 percent of 100 of all the blessings God gave me. From the time I was born I was blessed with full working organs and had all the body parts a human supposed to have. That's a billion and one blessings. So what makes you think 1 blessing or 1 prayer isn't going to work especially if God sees you struggling. Being raised by a depressed single mother is why He guided my conscience and made me physically and mentally instinct to things I never learned. That's how I know I was blessed. Also I grew up in a city where the more gun shots you hear, the less birthday cakes they make. No bullets ever touched me, only an angel when gun powder lingered the air. That's how I know I was being blessed. I lived in an era where if you don't spend time with your child the internet or the video games will. God saw that I was uncoached and He blessed me with godly instincts. Somewhere in my life, I 've been unloved, mistreated, cheated, lied to, pushed around, teased, bullied, full of anger, suicidal, but I am still here because I was able to recognize and control the thoughts that flow through my mind.

While God is giving me chances to better my life every day, I live for special moments. Moments become memories that maintain a smile on your face. This is why I enjoy every family member that I have. They are there to put a moment in your life so that you can have something to smile for when you get old. It's like a 401k plan except it last forever. Think of the elderly, what makes them to continue to smile; certainly not the doctors. A person that has nothing good to remember has already died mentally. I want to live long mentally and physically, and family and internal knowledge is the key ingredient for long life. Take Note: When I first played Pop Warner football at my first game, my mom showed up and cheered for me. Not only she was the loudest cheerleader, she was also my biggest fan. I remember when I sacked the quarterback, she cheered so much (was so happy) that other people on the sidelines thought she was nuts. She was running up and down the field cheering for me and sometimes I couldn't hear the quarterback hiking the ball because my mom was so loud. Even though she miss the rest of my games, that was one of the greatest moment I ever had. On my 3rd year of Pop Warner football, we played my grandfather home team (Roselle rams) and we (Elizabeth Pal) took a bus to arrive there. When we got there we warmed up and played. I only played the first quarter and didn't play anymore. There were so many players on our team that the coaches had to obey the rules (minimum of 8 plays for each player). Well soon after I played my grandfather came to the game on his bike. I was shock, proud and embarrassed all in one. I was shock because I didn't expect him to come, I was proud because he was there and I was embarrassed because I was on the bench. He asked me how come I wasn't in the game and I had to sadly tell him I played already. I wanted him to see me tackle somebody or catch the ball but I was unlucky that day. But my grandfather being there at my football game was one of the greatest moments in my life and now those memories will lengthen my life expectancy. Another beautiful moment I had is when my cousin Gel (Gerald) author of "Undivided We Fall" came to visit me and he saw that I was a writer when my mom showed him my sample book. He immediately saw something in me that I didn't see. He inspired and desired me to be a writer and continue to write. Though I really wasn't serious about writing books but the information he shared with me was heavenly sent. After he spoke to me, I've written over 40 books in 2 years. Just that 2 hour conversation he had with me created those 40 books and made me see opportunities that seemed invisible; that was a beautiful moment. Moments are beautiful things that strengthen your mental health and will lengthen your days. It becomes memories that you can never forget and I thank God for blessing me to have more beautiful moments.